Vocabulary Explorations

Level **A**

Lesli J. Favor, Ph.D.

Steven L. Stern

AMSCO

Amsco School Publications, Inc.
315 Hudson Street, New York, N.Y. 10013

About the Authors

Lesli J. Favor

Lesli J. Favor holds a Ph.D. in English from the University of North Texas. After graduating, she was assistant professor of English at Sul Ross State University Rio Grande College, in southwest Texas. She left that position to write full-time for publishers of books for school classrooms and libraries. She is the author of twenty English/language arts and nonfiction texts, in addition to coauthoring this three-volume vocabulary series. She lives near Seattle with her husband, young son, two dogs, and horse.

Steven L. Stern

Steven L. Stern has more than 30 years of experience as a writer and textbook editor, developing a wide range of books, educational products, and informational materials for children and adults. He has written many test-preparation books and is the author of two novels as well as numerous articles and short stories. He has also worked as an English teacher, a lexicographer, and a writing consultant. Mr. Stern lives in New Jersey.

Reviewers:

Jessica Bennett, Language Arts Teacher, Brookpark Middle School, and Membership
  Co-Chair, Ohio Council of Teachers of English Language Arts, Columbus, Ohio

Elizabeth Henley, Language Arts Teacher, Ardsley Middle School, Ardsley, New York

Julia Shepherd, Language Arts and History Teacher, Arizona Middle School, Riverside, California

Cover Design: Nesbitt Graphics, Inc.
Text Design and Composition: Nesbitt Graphics, Inc.
Cartoons: Angela Martini

Please visit our Web site at: *www.amscopub.com*

When ordering this book, please specify:
either **R 055 W** *or* VOCABULARY EXPLORATIONS, LEVEL A

ISBN: 978-1-56765-192-8
NYC Item 56765-192-7

Copyright © 2010 by Amsco School Publications, Inc.

Printed in the United States of America

1 2 3 4 5 6 7 8 9 10   15 14 13 12 11 10 09

Contents

Learning New and Special Words 109

Learning Words from Context 133

Thinking About Different Word Meanings 169

Understanding Shades of Meaning   201

Why and How to Use This Book

Why Vocabulary?

This book will help you expand your vocabulary and learn to think about words in different ways. But why does that matter?

Having a strong vocabulary will help you communicate with people. Imagine that a friend asks you about your day. If you say that it was "fine," your friend will get a hint of what your day was like. But if you use a more specific word, like "routine," "tiring," or "fantastic," your friend will get a sharper picture of what you experienced. A larger vocabulary helps you communicate more clearly so that people can better understand your thoughts and ideas.

Using the right words also gives you power. If you want to write a successful job application or a convincing article or letter, choosing exact words will help your voice be heard.

The more words you know, the more you'll be able to read and understand in your daily life. You'll gain greater meaning from books, magazines, newspapers, and Web sites, and you'll develop a deeper understanding of issues in the world around you.

Increasing your vocabulary will improve your writing, reading, and speaking, in school and beyond. *Vocabulary Explorations* will help get you there.

About This Series

This is the first book of **The Amsco Vocabulary Program**, a complete line of vocabulary books for middle and high school students. In *Vocabulary Explorations*, **Levels A–C**, you'll awaken your knowledge of words. You'll study how words come into our language, how to figure out and understand meanings, and how to know which words to use. In *Vocabulary for the High School Student*, you'll sharpen your knowledge of word parts and increase your vocabulary. In *Vocabulary for the College-Bound Student*, you'll learn more challenging words that will help you tackle college-level readings and textbooks. Note that every book in The Amsco Vocabulary Program contains practice sections to help you prepare for vocabulary questions on state tests and on national tests like the PSAT, SAT, and ACT.

What's Inside This Book

Here in *Vocabulary Explorations, Level A* you will find a variety of lessons, features, and activities.

> **Sneak Peek: Preview the Lesson:** This quick activity will get you thinking about the topic of the mini-lesson.

> **Vocabulary Mini-Lessons:** These lessons introduce key vocabulary concepts and provide examples. The first lessons focus on word parts (prefixes, suffixes, roots) and building words. The next lessons explore the other ways words come into general use, crossing over from mythology, foreign languages, and technology into everyday speech and writing. In the last lessons, you'll focus on word meanings. How can you figure out the definitions of new words? What if a word has more than one meaning?

> **Words to Know: Lists and Activities:** In each chapter, you'll find two or more word lists. Each list contains five or ten vocabulary words and their meanings, as well as sample sentences. You're also given the pronunciation of each word (called the phonetic respelling because it helps you sound it out). After the word lists are three kinds of activities.

>> **Own It: Develop Your Word Understanding** helps you understand the meanings of the new words.

>> **Link It: Make Word-to-World Connections** has you make a personal connection to the words and learn how to use them in your own life.

>> **Master It: Use Words in Meaningful Ways** has you try using your new words in different ways.

> **Wrapping Up: Review What You've Learned.** This section summarizes what you've learned in the chapter.

> **Flaunt It: Show Your Word Understanding.** These exercises help you review the words in each chapter. The exercises will help you prepare for state and national tests.

> **Activities à la Carte: Extend Your Word Knowledge.** At the end of each chapter, you'll find these creative extension activities from which you or your teacher can choose. There's also an **ELL** option.

Oh, and one more thing. As you work through the book, you'll be greeted by **Word Master Mike**, who will use some of the vocabulary words to tell you about his own life. As he does so, you'll gain a better sense of how you, too, can use these words.

Hey, I'm Word Master Mike. I love learning new words and using them to talk about stuff in school and in my life. A bigger vocabulary gives me more ways to express myself. As you work through this book, I'll be appearing here and there to tell you a bit about my life, using new words from each chapter. Good luck!

This book is an important resource that will increase your knowledge and understanding of words. Continue with the rest of The Amsco Vocabulary Program, and you'll see big improvements in your ability to speak and write effectively.

Good luck!
Lesli J. Favor, Ph.D. and Steven L. Stern, *Authors*
Lauren Davis, *Editor*

Learning Words Through Prefixes

1

Have you ever tried to put together a jigsaw puzzle? Have you ever pieced together train tracks, model airplanes, or bead jewelry? As you may have realized, in school and at play, we often encounter *pieces* that make up a whole.

Words are no different. Many of them are made up of parts that fit together like puzzle pieces. Once the parts are joined, the word's meaning is "whole," or complete. The parts of words include **base words** or **roots** (the *main* parts), **prefixes** (parts added to the *beginning* of base words or roots), and **suffixes** (parts added to the *end* of base words or roots). In this chapter, we'll focus on **prefixes**, which are added to the beginning of a word. You'll learn a variety of common prefixes, and you'll add to your vocabulary a number of words that begin with these prefixes.

In this chapter, you will learn
> What a prefix is
> How and why to add prefixes
> Words with Greek, Latin, and Anglo-Saxon prefixes

Sneak Peek: Preview the Lesson

Prefix Brainstorm

The chart on the next page contains some of the prefixes that you'll study in this lesson. With a partner, read the prefixes. Then, together, brainstorm for words you already know that use these prefixes. Write the words in the space provided. Once you've finished, share the results with your class. Your teacher may ask you to explain the meaning of one or more words that you list.

Prefixes

ex-	in-	re-	sub-
anti-	tele-	mis-	un-

Words I Know That Use These Prefixes

ocabulary Mini-Lesson: All About Prefixes

A **prefix** is a group of letters added to the beginning of a base word (a basic word) or a root (the main part of a word) to create a new word. Every prefix has a meaning. For example, the prefix *re-* means "back" or "again." What new words are created when you add *re-* to these base words?

PREFIX	+	BASE WORD	=	WORD
re-	+	pay	=	*repay* (to pay *back*)
re-	+	view	=	*review* (to view *again*)
re-	+	test	=	*retest* (to test *again*)

This time, instead of adding *re-*, let's add the prefix *pre-*, which means "before."

PREFIX	+	BASE WORD	=	WORD
pre-	+	pay	=	*prepay* (to pay *before*)
pre-	+	view	=	*preview* (to view *before*)
pre-	+	test	=	*pretest* (to test *before*)

By changing the prefix, you create new words.

> **Tip**
>
> Now that you know what *pre-* means, it'll be easier to remember what a *prefix* is. A *prefix* is something that is "fixed (attached) *before*" a word.

Unlike base words, which are complete, basic words (*pay, view, test*), roots are main word parts that usually cannot stand alone; they need another part to be complete. For example, a common root is *ject* ("to throw"); it is a *main word part* but it is not a complete word by itself.

Prefixes are added to roots the same way they're added to base words. Let's see how this is done by adding a prefix to two common roots—*ject*, "to throw," and *port*, which means "to carry." What words are formed by combining the prefix *re-* with these roots? (Remember that *re-* means "back" or "again.")

PREFIX	+	ROOT	=	WORD
re-	+	*port* (carry)	=	*report*
re-	+	*ject* (throw)	=	*reject*

Joining *re-* with *port* creates the word *report*, which technically means "to carry back." So when a teacher asks you to report on a topic, he or she is asking you to "carry back" information!

Joining *re-* with *ject* forms the word *reject*, which technically means "to throw back." See if you can figure out how something is "thrown back" in these two examples.

> Sarah offered me $10 for the book, but I decided to *reject* her offer.

> The producer *rejected* the actor for the part because he was too tall.

Why Learn This?

Knowing some common prefixes will help you figure out the meanings of unfamiliar words. When you learn a prefix, you have a clue to figuring out the meaning of every word that begins with that prefix. For example, you may know that the prefix *tri-* means three. That will help you understand many words, such as

> *triangle*: a figure with three angles and three sides
>
> *tricolor*: three colors, as in the *tricolor flag of France*
>
> *tricycle*: a three-wheeled bike
>
> *trio*: a group of three, as in a *singing trio*
>
> *triplets*: three children born at the same time

Knowing the meaning of *tri-* may not help you figure out *every* word that begins with it, but you'll at least have a good clue. For example, when you studied dinosaurs, you probably read about *triceratops*. Now that you know *tri-*, can you guess how many horns a triceratops had? And have you heard of a race called a *triathlon*? How many events are in a triathlon?

> ## Tip
>
> Look for prefixes in the world around you. A lot of the new words in our language were created by adding prefixes to familiar base words. For example, advertisements sell *preowned* cars—a fancy way of saying *used* cars. Food may be *undercooked* or *overcooked*.

Words to Know: Vocabulary Lists and Activities

Most prefixes in the English language come from Latin, Greek, or Anglo-Saxon (Old English). In the word lists you are about to study, you will see examples of all three.

Here are a few things to keep in mind.

> A prefix may have just one meaning (*tri-* means "three"), or it may have more than one (*re-* means "back" or "again").

> Two different prefixes can have the same meaning. For example, the Latin prefix *in-*, as in *invisible*, and the Anglo-Saxon prefix *un-*, as in *unbelievable*, both mean "not."

> Some prefixes are spelled in more than one way. For example, the prefix *com-* means "together," as in *committee*. The prefix may also be spelled *con-*, as in *connect*.

> Some words have more than one prefix. For example, *unreported* ("not carried back") has *un-* ("not") and *re-* ("back").

List 1   Words with Latin Prefixes

Study these four Latin prefixes. Then read the table of words that are formed with these prefixes. Read each word, what it means, and how it's used.

Prefix	Meaning	Examples
com-, con-	together or with	**com**pose, **con**tract, **con**tribute
e-, ex-	out; from; away	**e**rupt, **ex**hale
in-	not or the opposite of	**in**accurate, **in**active, **in**formal
inter-	between or among	**inter**fere, **inter**national

Word	What It Means	How It's Used
compose *(v)* come-POZE	to form by putting *together*	The musician felt inspired to *compose* a love song.
contract *(n)* KON-trakt	an agreement between two or more people (literally, "draw *together*")	The basketball player signed a two-year *contract* with the team.
contribute *(v)* kon-TRIH-byoot	to give *together*	Parents were asked to *contribute* money to buy books for the school library.
erupt *(v)* e-RUHPT	to burst forth (literally, "to break *out*")	When the volcano *erupted*, steaming lava poured out.
exhale *(v)* eks-HAYL	to breathe *out*	Kim took a deep breath and then slowly *exhaled*.
inaccurate *(adj)* in-AK-yer-it	*not* accurate; incorrect	This news story is *inaccurate* because the reporter did not check his facts.
inactive *(adj)* in-AK-tiv	*not* active or moving	Cats are usually *inactive* in the afternoon and take a nap.
informal *(adj)* in—FAWR-muhl	*not* formal; casual; relaxed	"What's up?" is an *informal* greeting.
interfere *(v)* in-ter-FEER	to come *between*; get involved in the business of others	My cousins are having an argument, but I think it's best not to *interfere*.
international *(adj)* in-ter-NASH-uh-nl	*between* or *among* nations	The United States and China signed an *international* trade agreement.

Own It: Develop Your Word Understanding

Prefix Wheels

Directions: Work with a partner on this activity. For each Prefix Wheel on the next two pages, complete these steps:

1. Fill in the Prefix Wheel by writing the meaning of each word in the space provided.

2. Complete each sentence or answer the question printed beneath the wheel. Use your knowledge of the key word to decide how to respond.

3. *Bonus:* In the blank section of the wheel, write additional words you know that begin with the given prefix or prefixes.

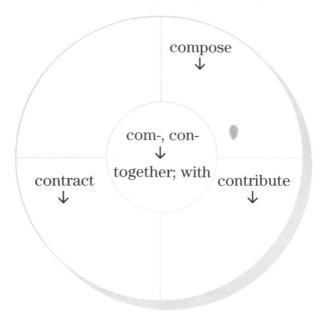

Something that you have **composed** is _____

How can you **contribute** to a cleaner school? _____

_____

An actor might sign a **contract** promising to _____

_____

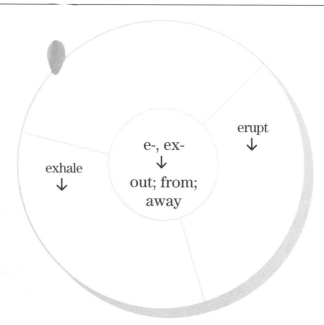

Which could be said to **erupt**: a person's kindness or a person's anger? _____

Which of these cannot **exhale**? dog mouse doll child

(circle one)

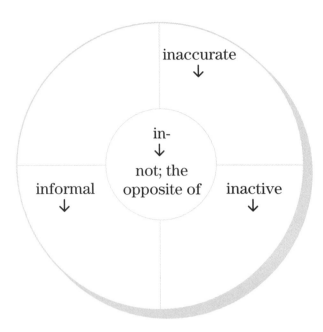

An **inaccurate** idea that someone has about you is _____

_____

When are you usually **inactive**—morning, afternoon, or night?
(circle one)

Which clothing style is **informal**—tuxedo pants or denim shorts?
(circle one)

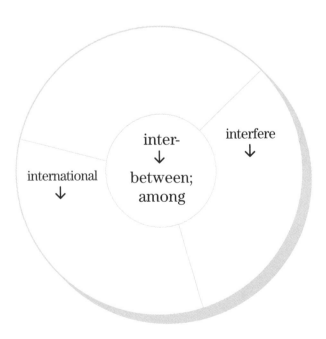

Which is more welcome—assistance or **interference**?
(circle one)

An **international** sporting event is _____

Link It: Make Word-to-World Connections

Person, Place, or Thing?

Directions: Follow these steps to complete the activity.

1. Read each word in the first column of the table below.
2. In the second column, complete the sentence *This word makes me think of . . .* by writing the name of a person, place, or thing.
3. In the third column, write a sentence or two explaining the connection. Try to use the key word in your explanation.

A sample response for *compose* is completed for you.

This word . . .	. . . makes me think of . . .	Sentence
compose	Trevor.	My cousin Trevor likes to compose music.
1. compose		
2. contribute		
3. contract		
4. erupt		
5. exhale		
6. inaccurate		
7. inactive		
8. informal		
9. interfere		
10. international		

I love sports, but I don't like having phys. ed. first period. It would be <u>inaccurate</u> to say that I am a morning person. I'm pretty sleepy and <u>inactive</u> in the mornings, so I don't <u>contribute</u> much to the games our teacher makes us play.

Master It: Use Words in Meaningful Ways

The Price of Fame

Directions: Follow these steps to complete the activity. Write your answers on your own paper.

1. With your classmates, brainstorm a list of famous people who are often in the public eye—in other words, everything they do is publicized on TV, in newspapers, in magazines, and on the Web. These people may include professional athletes, actors, musicians, and politicians.

2. Choose one of the people listed in step 1. Imagine what it must be like for this person to live in the public eye. Consider issues such as press coverage, money, privacy, and so on. Jot down some of your ideas.

3. Write a paragraph describing "the price of fame" for the person you chose. Use as many vocabulary words from List 1 (page 4) as you can in your paragraph.

List 2   Words with Latin Prefixes

Study the four new Latin prefixes that follow and ten words that use these prefixes. Read each word, what it means, and how it's used.

Prefix	Meaning	Examples
pro-	before or forward	**pro**claim, **pro**mote, **pro**voke
re-	back or again	**re**assure, **re**verse, **re**vive
sub-	under or below	**sub**marine, **sub**merge
trans-	across	**trans**mit, **trans**parent

Word	What It Means	How It's Used
proclaim (v) proh-KLAME	to declare publicly (literally, "to cry out *before*")	The colonies *proclaimed* their independence from England.
promote (v) pruh-MOHT	to raise in position or rank (literally, "to move *forward*")	After two years on the job, Max was *promoted* to assistant manager.
provoke (v) pruh-VOHK	to stir up; bring forth; cause (literally, "to call *forward*")	Ashley's story *provoked* laughter from her classmates.
reassure (v) ree-uh-SHUR	to assure *again*; give confidence to	The child was scared, but his parents *reassured* him that there were no monsters in the closet.
reverse (adj) ri-VURS	opposite in position or direction (literally, "turned *backward*")	Can you say the letters of the alphabet in *reverse* order?
revive (v) ri-VIVE	to bring *back* to life or consciousness (literally, "to make alive *again*")	The swimmer nearly drowned, but the lifeguard was able to *revive* her.
submarine (n) suhb-muh-REEN	a vessel designed to operate *under* water (*mare* is Latin for "sea")	Most *submarines* are used as naval ships, but some do scientific research.
submerge (v) suhb-MURJ	to put or go *under* water	Floodwaters threatened to *submerge* the town.
transmit (v) trans-MIT	to send or pass from one place or person to another (literally, "to send *across*")	Scientists are *transmitting* messages into space in hopes of finding intelligent life.
transparent (adj) trans-PAR-uhnt	letting light through so that objects on the other side can be seen	A windowpane is made of *transparent* glass.

Own It: Develop Your Word Understanding

Just Say It!

Directions: Work in a group of four people to complete the activity. Follow these steps:

1. Assign each person one of the prefixes used in the word list (*pro-*, *re-*, *sub-*, and *trans-*).

2. On one side of an index card or sheet of paper, print your assigned prefix in large block letters. On the other side, write each word from List 2 (page 10) that uses the prefix.

3. Quietly, practice saying each of your words aloud. Think about ways to use each word to describe or tell something about yourself. (For example, The music awards show *revived* my desire to become a famous singer.)

4. Hold up your index card to show the group your prefix. Say the prefix. Then read each of your words aloud. After reading each word, use it in a positive description or statement about yourself.

In music class, when I <u>proclaimed</u> that I was a better singer than Zac Efron (of *High School Musical*), my comment <u>provoked</u> laughter and <u>revived</u> everyone who had been falling asleep at their desks. If you have to ask why that was so funny, then you've never heard me...

Link It: Make Word-to-World Connections

Movie Poster

Directions: In this activity, you will create a movie poster that shows your knowledge of the vocabulary words. Follow these steps:

1. Gather materials to create a poster about a movie you like. You'll need poster board or other large paper to serve as the poster

form. You'll also need magazine cutouts, photocopies, your own artwork, paints, pens, or similar supplies.

2. Plan your poster. Besides planning images, think about how you can use many or all of the List 2 vocabulary words. For example, you could make up one-line movie reviews, a statement telling about the plot, or quotations from the actors.

3. Create the movie poster. Display your poster in class and point out the ways you used the vocabulary words to tell people about the movie.

Master It: Use Words in Meaningful Ways

Concise Writing

Read the sentence in each item below. Replace each underlined phrase with a vocabulary word from List 2 (page 10). Write your new sentence on separate paper. The first one has been done for you.

1. It was totally embarrassing when he <u>declared out loud</u> his love for me over the loudspeaker.

   It was totally embarrassing when he proclaimed his love for me over the loudspeaker.

2. My mom's boss decided to <u>give a higher position to</u> her.

3. When the band cancelled the concert, they didn't realize it would <u>bring about</u> so much anger from their fans.

4. Even though Erik tried to <u>give comfort to</u> Tara, she was still upset about the grade.

5. Jerry is wearing his shirt in <u>a backwards way</u>.

6. The actress wasn't getting much publicity for a while, but her new movie is sure to <u>bring back</u> her career.

7. I saw the <u>underwater vessel</u> return to the water's surface.

8. The water is freezing, but once you <u>put underwater</u> your head, you'll get used to it.

9. If you go to school with the flu, you might <u>pass along</u> your germs to others.

10. The windows of the limo were not <u>allowing light through</u>, so I couldn't tell which celebrity was inside.

List 3 Words with Greek Prefixes

Here are four Greek prefixes and some common words that are formed with them. Read each word, what it means, and how it's used.

Prefix	Meaning	Examples
anti-	against	**anti**freeze, **anti**war
auto-	self	**auto**biography, **auto**graph, **auto**matic
dia-	across or through	**dia**gonal, **dia**logue, **dia**meter
tele-	distant; far	**tele**communication, **tele**scope

Word	What It Means	How It's Used
antifreeze *(n)* AN-ti-freez	a substance added to a liquid to keep it from freezing	Be sure to add *antifreeze* to your car's radiator if you live in a cold climate.
antiwar *(adj)* AN-ti-wawr	*against* war or against a particular war	*Antiwar* protesters marched in Washington to convey their feelings to the president.
autobiography *(n)* aw-tuh-by-AH-gruh-fee	a person's biography (life story) written by the person him*self* or her*self*	Reading this celebrity's *autobiography* helped me understand her feelings about fame.
autograph *(n)* AW-tuh-graf	a person's handwritten signature	The baseball player gave me his *autograph* on the ball I caught.
automatic *(adj)* aw-tuh-MAT-ik	acting or moving by it*self*	My new camera has an *automatic* focus feature.
diagonal *(n)* die-AG-uh-nl	extending on a slant between opposite points	Points A and B in this chart are connected by a *diagonal* line.
dialogue *(n)* DAHY-uh-lawg	a conversation between two or more people (literally, "to speak *across*")	When I revised my story, I added more *dialogue* to show the characters speaking.

continued

diameter *(n)* die-AM-i-ter	a straight line passing *through* the center of a circle from one side to the other	The *diameter* divides a circle into two halves.
telecommunication *(n)* tel-i-kuh-myoo-ni-KAY-shuhn	electronic communication over long *distances*	Wireless computers and cell phones are two present-day examples of *telecommunication*.
telescope *(n)* TEL-uh-skohp	instrument for viewing *distant* objects	Astronomers use powerful *telescopes* to study objects in space.

Own It: Develop Your Word Understanding

Prefix Matchup

Directions: In this activity, you will be given a prefix *or* a root or base word. Your job is to find a classmate who has the other half of your word. Here's how the activity works:

1. Your teacher will write each vocabulary word from List 3 on an index card and then cut the cards in half so that the prefix is on one half, and the base word or root is on the other half. Your teacher will jumble the cards together in a box.

2. Each student will take one card from the box.

3. Move around the classroom to find the person who has the other half of your word. When you find that person, practice saying the complete word aloud. Write the word (using correct spelling!) on a sheet of paper and review the word's meaning.

4. When everyone has found a word partner, share the results. One of you reads the word aloud to the class. The other person states the word's meaning.

Link It: Make Word-to-World Connections

Act Out in Class

Directions: In this activity, you will act out a demonstration of a word's meaning. For example, to act out the meaning of *antiwar*, you might write *war* inside a circle, slash a line across it signaling "no," and walk around with the sign held high. Follow these steps to complete the activity:

1. Choose a word from the vocabulary list (pages 13–14) that you want to act out. If you need a partner for your act, get permission to pair up for the activity.

2. Spend about five minutes planning and practicing your act. Make sure that your act gives clues to the meaning of the vocabulary word *without* writing or stating the word directly.

3. Act out your word for the class and let your classmates try to guess the word.

Master It: Use Words in Meaningful Ways

Did You Know?

Directions: In this activity, you will choose one vocabulary word to explore further. Then you'll share a few facts about this word with your classmates. Follow these steps:

1. Review the list of vocabulary words and their meanings on pages 13–14. Choose one word that you find interesting.

2. Find **two or three** facts about the word that you can share with your class. For instance, what's the difference between an *autobiography* and a biography? What is the *diameter* of a quarter? Useful sources of information include textbooks, encyclopedias, friends, family members, and magazine articles.

3. Write a few sentences stating two or three facts about the vocabulary word. Here are some phrases that you could use to begin the sentences:

> Did you know that . . .

> A surprising fact about (*vocabulary word*) is . . .

> A question I had about (*vocabulary word*) was . . .

4. Practice reading your sentences aloud. Then read your sentences to your classmates.

List 4 Words with Anglo-Saxon Prefixes

You've studied Latin and Greek prefixes; now let's look at some common Anglo-Saxon ones. Study these four Anglo-Saxon prefixes and ten words that contain them. Read each word, what it means, and how it's used.

Prefix	Meaning	Examples
a-	on; in; in a state	**a**board, **a**float, **a**shore
mis-	wrong; wrongly	**mis**behave, **mis**pronounce
un-	not or the opposite of	**un**conscious, **un**solved, **un**welcome
under-	too little; not enough	**under**estimate, **under**pay

Word	What It Means	How It's Used
aboard *(adv)* uh-BAWRD	*on* a ship, airplane, or other vehicle	The flight attendant greeted us as we walked *aboard* the plane.
afloat *(adv)* uh-FLOHT	floating	It was amazing that the sailboat stayed *afloat* during the storm.
ashore *(adv)* uh-SHOR	to or *on* the shore	We anchored our boat and swam *ashore*.
misbehave *(v)* mis-bi-HAYV	to behave badly	Mom punished Colin because he *misbehaved*.
mispronounce *(v)* mis-pruh-NOWNCE	to pronounce incorrectly	If you say the word *picture* as "pit-cher," you are *mispronouncing* it.
unconscious *(adj)* uhn-KON-shuss	*not* conscious or aware	A blow to the head left the football player *unconscious*.
unsolved *(adj)* uhn-SAHL-ved	*not* solved; without explanation	The detective worked hard, but the crime remained *unsolved*.
unwelcome *(adj)* uhn-WELL-kuhm	*not* wanted or welcome	Ants are *unwelcome* guests at a picnic.
underestimate *(v)* uhn-der-ES-tuh-mayt	to estimate too low; place too low a value on	When fans saw how well the basketball player handled the ball, they realized they had *underestimated* his abilities.
underpay *(v)* uhn-der-PAY	to pay *too little*	Emily felt that she had been *underpaid* for babysitting because the kids were so much work.

Own It: Develop Your Word Understanding

Draw It!

Directions: In this activity, you will *draw* simple sketches that will help you remember the meaning of each word. Follow these steps:

1. Study the list above of vocabulary words and definitions.
2. Write a different vocabulary word in each box in the organizer. Practice saying the word aloud.
3. Draw a simple picture that will help you remember the meaning of each word. For example, to remember *underestimate*,

you might draw a jar full of ten jelly beans. Then, to the side, write "estimate: 4 jelly beans."

4. When you have finished filling in the table, share your work with a classmate for further ideas and inspiration. Make any changes that you discover are needed.

My Memory Cues	
Word: Sketch	Word: Sketch
Word: Sketch	Word: Sketch
Word: Sketch	Word: Sketch
Word: Sketch	Word: Sketch
Word: Sketch	Word: Sketch

Link It: Make Word-to-World Connections

Rhythm

Directions: In this activity, you will work with classmates to create a rap, rhyme, or chant using some or all of the vocabulary words. Follow the steps on the top of the next page.

1. Form groups of four people.

2. Choose a rhythmic pattern to use. Examples include a military cadence such as "I don't know what you've been told," the rhythm of a familiar rap, and the singsong pattern of a nursery rhyme such as "Three Blind Mice."

3. Play around with the vocabulary words (on page 16), forming phrases or sentences and setting them to the rhythm. It's okay to be goofy—just make sure your use of each word makes sense. Use as many of the vocabulary words as you can.

4. Perform your group's creation for the class.

Master It: Use Words in Meaningful Ways

Summer Day Camp

Directions: Read the following advertisement for summer camp volunteers.

Lakeshore Day Camp Needs Volunteers!

Do your summer plans include swimming, playing games, and making new friends? They ought to! Why not spend part of your summer as a volunteer at Lakeshore Day Camp?

Located on the shores of beautiful Lake Pine, Lakeshore Day Camp provides fun, safe child care for children ages 5–10. We need summer volunteers to help with craft projects, paddleboats, sing-alongs, games, and refreshments.

If you will be age 12 or older this summer, we need YOU to volunteer! Volunteers will receive *free* CPR training, *free* swim lessons, *free* refreshments, and a *free* T-shirt.

Are you interested? Write us a letter explaining why you would make a great volunteer. Send your letter to this address:

Mr. Ralph Owens, Director of Volunteers

Lakeshore Day Camp

56 Lakeshore Road

Pine Valley, CO 81020

Be sure to mail your letter by April 30. We hope to hear from you soon!

Imagine that you want to volunteer at Lakeshore Day Camp. Write a letter to Mr. Owens, explaining why you would make a great volunteer. In your letter, use as many vocabulary words from the list on page 16 as you can. Underline each one.

Wrapping Up: Review What You've Learned

Here's a brief summary of what you've studied in this chapter.

> A **prefix** is a group of letters added to the beginning of a base word or root that changes its meaning or creates a new word.

> Most prefixes in the English language come from Latin, Greek, or Anglo-Saxon (Old English).

> A prefix may have one or more meanings. Two different prefixes can mean the same thing.

> Some prefixes are spelled in more than one way.

> Knowing prefixes can help you figure out the meanings of unfamiliar words.

> You learned the following prefixes and words that are formed with them.

com-, con- (together, with)

e-, ex- (out, from, or away)

in- (not or the opposite of)

inter- (between or among)

pro- (before or forward)

re- (back or again)

sub- (under or below)

trans- (across)

anti- (against)

auto- (self)

dia- (across or through)

tele- (distant or far)

a- (on; in; in a state)

mis- (wrong; wrongly)

un- (not or the opposite of)

under- (too little; not enough)

Chapter Review Exercises

Flaunt It: Show Your Word Understanding

In these exercises, you'll demonstrate your understanding of each vocabulary word. You will use vocabulary words, or forms of the words, to complete sentences and to write sentences of your own.

A Sentence Completion

Directions: Circle the letter of the word that best completes each sentence.

1. When Rachel caught me reading her diary, her anger _____.
   - **a.** exhaled
   - **b.** proclaimed
   - **c.** erupted
   - **d.** provoked

2. John Hancock's signature on the Declaration of Independence is perhaps our nation's most famous _____.
   - **a.** contract
   - **b.** autograph
   - **c.** autobiography
   - **d.** telecommunication

3. I had lost interest in drawing portraits, but Mrs. Hall's art class _____ my interest in this art form.
   - **a.** composed
   - **b.** interfered
   - **c.** submerged
   - **d.** revived

4. Jumping out of the canoe, Freddie pulled it _____ and tied it securely to a stake in the sand.
   - **a.** aboard
   - **b.** diagonal
   - **c.** ashore
   - **d.** afloat

5. This summer, the film's leading actors will go on a tour to _____ their movie to fans, critics, and the media.
   - **a.** promote
   - **b.** provoke
   - **c.** reassure
   - **d.** transmit

B Word Bank

Directions: Choose a word from the box to complete each sentence. Write the word on the line provided. Each word is used only once.

antifreeze	submarine	informally	telescope	underestimated
unsolved	reverse	unwelcome	inactive	international

6. The volcano is _____ now, but scientists say that it could become active at some time in the future.

7. To create the secret code, he wrote the letters of each word in _____ order.

8. At the _____ food fair, I tasted Japanese sushi, Indian curry chicken, Native American fry bread, and Mexican tacos.

9. My mom dresses in nice suits for work, but my dad dresses more _____ for his job as a bus driver.

10. Could you help me with these math problems that I left _____ on my homework sheet?

11. If you insist on burping every two minutes, then you are _____ at this dinner table.

12. The _____ moved away from the shore and then slowly submerged.

13. Unfortunately, I _____ how much time I would need to do my homework.

14. Tonight, let's use your _____ to study the surface of the moon.

15. At the auto supply store, we bought oil and _____ for our car.

(Writing

Directions: Follow the directions to write sentences using vocabulary words. Write your sentences on a separate sheet of paper.

16. Use *diameter* in a description of an object.

17. Use *misbehave* in a command spoken to children.

18. Use *underpay* in a statement about babysitters.

19. Use *transparent* to describe something in your bedroom.

20. Use *antiwar* to tell about someone's opinion.

21. Use *inaccurate* in a statement about someone's spelling.

22. Use *automatic* to tell about something in your kitchen.

23. Use *dialogue* to tell about a story.

24. Use *mispronounce* in a statement about a friend.

25. Use *unconscious* in a statement about a doctor.

Chapter Extension Activities

Activities à la Carte: Extend Your Word Knowledge

The activities on this page are presented à la carte, like items on a restaurant menu, meaning that you can choose from a variety of options. Your teacher may assign an activity or let you pick the one that tempts your appetite. If time allows, you might do more than one activity. All of the activities feature the same ingredient: **prefixes**. Dig in!

Notice Me!

Have you ever shopped for magazines? Chances are, you chose one with a cover headline that caught your eye. These headlines shout, "Notice me!" and bring in sales. With this in mind, create your own magazine cover on poster board. Choose a theme (sports, model airplanes, extraterrestrials, etc.) and use magazine cutouts or your own art. Then write attention-grabbing headlines. The challenge? Use at least one prefix in each headline.

I'm a Poet

Do you have the mind of a poet? Or do you just like to experiment with language? Use vocabulary words in this chapter to inspire a poem of your own. Feel free to throw in additional words that use prefixes. A rhyme pattern is optional!

Memory Game

Create a memory card game. You need ten index cards and a list of five words that have prefixes. Use two cards per word—on one card, write the prefix; on the other card, write the base word or root. Shuffle the cards and place them facedown in rows. Invite one or two friends to play. To begin, turn over a card. Then turn over another card. If the two cards form a word, you get a point. If the cards don't form a word, turn them facedown again. Then the next person gets a turn.

Before and After

Pre- is a prefix meaning "before," and *post-* is a prefix meaning "after." How many expressions can you create using these prefixes? Here are a few to get you started: pretest jitters, postgame party, prevacation excitement. Invent a few new words using these two prefixes.

Educational—and Tasty!

Invite a friend over and get out a box of alphabet cereal. See who can be the first to use cereal to spell three words with prefixes. You may eat your results.

You're Invited

Use prefixes to lure friends to your house. How? Create a flyer to tempt them with a favorite activity—and use prefixes! For instance, you could write, "**Re**new your interest in sleepovers!" or "An **in**formal pizza party—You're **in**vited!" Then write the details of when and where. Make copies of the flyer and give them to your closest friends. Prepare to **en**joy yourself!

¿Hablas español? Parlez-vous français?

Do you speak a language other than English? Compare the use of prefixes in that language to what you have learned about English prefixes. You could start by translating some of the vocabulary words in this chapter. Answer such questions as, "Do the two languages use the same or similar prefixes?"

Misbehaving with Words

Explore the value of prefixes by finding phrases and sentences in your everyday world to "misbehave" with. Look at signs, headlines, titles, menus, logos, and more. Remove, replace, or add prefixes to create an entirely new—and sometimes wacky—idea. For example, the headline "Teen Bicycle Race" becomes "Teen Tricycle Race." Read some of the "before" and "after" expressions to your class.

Learning Words Through Suffixes

2

You've probably heard the expression "last but not least." It reminds us that being last does not mean being least important. The same idea applies to word parts. A **suffix** is a part added to the end of a word. Even though the suffix comes last, it is just as important as other parts in forming a word's meaning. In this chapter, you'll learn how to identify various types of suffixes and how to use these word parts to get meaning from words you read.

Objectives

In this chapter, you will learn
> What a suffix is
> How and why to add suffixes
> Words with noun, verb, adjective, and adverb suffixes

Sneak Peek: Preview the Lesson

What I Know Already

In the diagram on the next page, fill in what you know already about suffixes. Do your best to complete the diagram without looking at the lesson that follows. It's okay if you leave blank spaces. If that happens, you'll know what information to study closely as you complete the lesson.

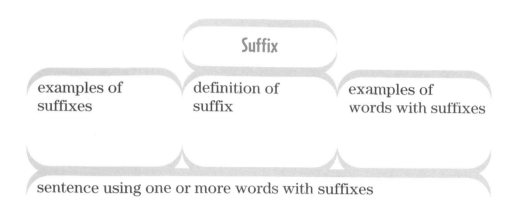

Suffix

- examples of suffixes
- definition of suffix
- examples of words with suffixes

sentence using one or more words with suffixes

Ⓥocabulary Mini-Lesson: All About Suffixes

Prefixes are word parts attached to the *beginning* of words, but suffixes are word parts attached to the *end*. A **suffix** is a group of letters added to the end of a base word or root that changes its meaning or creates a new word.

Each suffix has its own meaning. For example, the suffix *-less* means "without." When you add *-less* to the following base words, what new words do you have?

BASE WORD	+	SUFFIX	= WORD
hope	+	*-less*	= *hopeless* (*without* hope)
fear	+	*-less*	= *fearless* (*without* fear)
use	+	*-less*	= *useless* (*without* use)

The suffix *-ful* has the opposite meaning of *-less*. It means "full of" or "having." Try adding *-ful* to the same three base words.

BASE WORD	+	SUFFIX	= WORD
hope	+	*-ful*	= *hopeful* (*full of* hope)
fear	+	*-ful*	= *fearful* (*having* fear)
use	+	*-ful*	= *useful* (*having* use)

Do you see how suffixes can affect a word's meaning? *Fear* means being afraid, but if you add *-less*, you get *fearless* which means "not afraid"!

Now let's add suffixes to roots. The suffix *-fy* means "to make." Let's add it to two Latin roots.

ROOT	+	SUFFIX	= WORD
clar (clear)	+	*-(i)fy*	= *clarify* (*to make* clear)

The teacher's explanation will *clarify* the poem's meaning.

cert (sure)	+	*-(i)fy*	= *certify* (*to make* sure or certain)

This document will *certify* my date of birth.

Did You Know?

Many words have more than one suffix. Here are some examples.

carelessness = *care* + *-less* + *-ness*

humorously = *humor* + *-ous* + *-ly*

cheerfully = *cheer* + *-ful* + *-ly*

What others can you think of?

Why Learn This?

Learning suffixes can help your reading comprehension. Suffixes often give you a clue about a word's part of speech, and knowing a word's part of speech can help you understand a sentence you're reading. For example, words ending in the suffix *-ment* are usually nouns—names of people, places, things, or ideas. *Govern<u>ment</u>* and *entertain<u>ment</u>* are two examples. Similarly, many words ending in *-ly* are adverbs—words that describe verbs, adjectives, or other adverbs. *Careless<u>ly</u>* and *mysterious<u>ly</u>* are examples.

When you know a word's part of speech, you can see how the word relates to other words in the sentence. This helps you understand the sentence better. Look at these examples:

The *playful* puppy grabbed the ball and ran away.

(*Playful* is an adjective, describing the noun *puppy*.)

The puppy *playfully* grabbed the ball and ran away.

(*Playfully* is an adverb, describing how the puppy *grabbed* [verb] the ball.)

Even if you didn't know what *playfully* means, you could use your knowledge of the suffix *-ly* to figure out that it's an adverb and is somehow describing the puppy's action.

Quick Review: The Parts of Speech

Suffixes help you identify these parts of speech:

noun   names a person, place, thing, or idea
                  Examples: woman, country, computer, peace

verb   expresses action
                  Examples: run, talk, study

adjective   describes a noun or a pronoun
                  Examples: tall, blue, wise

adverb   describes a verb but may also describe an
                  adjective or another adverb
                  Examples: slowly, secretly

Knowing suffixes helps you as a writer, too. If you change the suffix on a word, then you can use that word in a different way. Here are some examples.

From verb to noun: govern + -*ment* = government
From adjective to verb: sharp + -*en* = sharpen
From noun to adjective: joy + -*less* = joyless
From adjective to adverb: natural + -*ly* = naturally

You can write that a character felt *joy* over being asked out by her crush, or you can write that the character *joyfully* said yes.

Words to Know: Vocabulary Lists and Activities

In Chapter 1, the prefixes you studied were grouped according to their language of origin: Latin, Greek, or Anglo-Saxon. Suffixes also come from different languages, and many English words combine suffixes from one language with roots and prefixes from other languages. Rather than focus on their origin, however, this chapter groups suffixes by the part of speech they usually show: noun, verb, adjective, and adverb. This grouping will help you learn *how to use* these suffixes.

When you study the following word lists, remember these points:

> A suffix may have more than one meaning. The suffix -*ment*, for example, can refer to a "process" or a "result." Compare these sentences:

The *development* of modern farming methods took many years.

(*process* of developing)

Kayla's mistake caused her great *embarrassment*.

(*result* of being embarrassed)

> Two different suffixes can have the same meaning. For instance, *-ful* and *-ous* both mean "full of," as in *joyful* and *joyous*.

> Some suffixes are spelled in more than one way. For example, *-ic* and *-ical* are two forms of the same suffix, meaning "relating to," as in *historic/historical* and *rhythmic/rhythmical*.

> When a suffix is added to a base word, the word may stay the same, or letters may be dropped, added, or changed. Here are a few examples:

cheer + *-ful* = cheer*ful* (no spelling change)

argue + *-ment* = argu*ment* (the *e* is dropped)

happy + *-ly* = happi*ly* (*y* changes to *i*)

You'll learn more about these spelling changes in Chapter 4.

List 5   Words with Noun Suffixes

Here are some common suffixes that form nouns—names of people, places, things, or ideas. Study these suffixes and the ten words (all nouns) that are formed with them. Read each word, its meaning, and how it's used.

Suffix	Meaning	Examples
-ant, -ent	person or thing that	immigr**ant**, inhabit**ant**, resid**ent**
-dom	state or condition	bore**dom**, free**dom**
-er, -or	person who	manag**er**, narrat**or**
-ment	condition of being, or action, process, or result	amaze**ment**, encourage**ment**, judg**ment**

Word	What It Means	How It's Used
immigrant *(n)* IM-ih-grant	a *person who* immigrates (comes to a new country)	Many *immigrants* from Europe settled in the United States.
inhabitant *(n)* in-HAB-i-tuhnt	a *person or animal that* inhabits (lives in) a place	Bears and coyotes are *inhabitants* of this forest.

continued

resident *(n)* REZ-i-duhnt	*a person who* resides (lives in) a place	You must be a *resident* of this town to vote in local elections.
boredom *(n)* BOAR-duhm	*state or condition* of being bored	To relieve his *boredom*, Mike played a video game.
freedom *(n)* FREE-duhm	*state or condition* of being free	People fought for their *freedom* during the American Revolution.
manager *(n)* MAN-i-jer	*person who* manages	The store *manager* interviewed Lauren for a part-time job.
narrator *(n)* NAR-ay-ter	*person who* narrates (tells a story)	The *narrator* of this story is a young woman from China.
amazement *(n)* uh-MAYZ-ment	*condition of being* amazed or surprised	We stood there in *amazement*, staring at the little green man.
encouragement *(n)* en-KUR-ij-ment	*action* of encouraging or inspiring	Teachers offer *encouragement* to students to help them do well.
judgment *(n)* JUHJ-ment	*result* of judging	In my *judgment*, dogs make the best pets.

Own It: Develop Your Word Understanding

Suffix Organizers

Directions: Work with a partner. Each of you completes two of the following four graphic organizers. Then share your results. For each organizer, follow these steps:

1. *Top:* Read the suffixes in the top box.
2. *Middle:* In the "used in" box, write the vocabulary words that use the given suffix(es). In the "meaning" box, write the meaning of the suffix(es). In the "memory cue" box, sketch or write a clue to help you remember the suffix's meaning.
3. *Bottom:* Use your knowledge of each key word to complete the sentences.

-ant, -ent

used in	meaning	memory cue

I might study *immigrants* in this school subject: _____
I am an *inhabitant* of _____
I am a *resident* of _____

-dom

used in	meaning	memory cue

I am overcome with *boredom* when I have to _____
_____
The U.S. Civil War resulted in *freedom* for _____

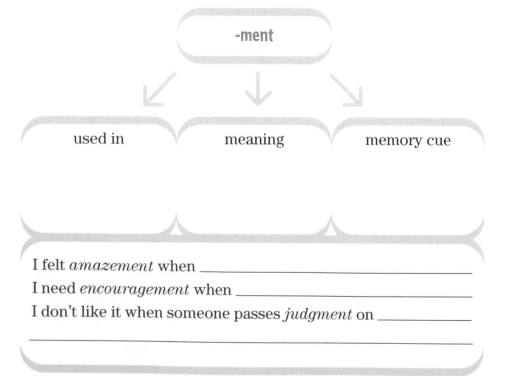

-er, -or

| used in | meaning | memory cue |

A *manager* might work in _____

In a work of fiction, the *narrator* _____

-ment

| used in | meaning | memory cue |

I felt *amazement* when _____

I need *encouragement* when _____

I don't like it when someone passes *judgment* on _____

_____

Link It: Make Word-to-World Connections

All About Us

Directions: Your assignment is to create a poster about your family or your "family" of friends. You can work alone or with a partner. Here's what to do:

1. Study the list of vocabulary words (pages 29–30). Think about ways these words connect to you and your family or friends. Perhaps you can use the words to make statements (inform), to express hopes and dreams, or to describe people. Write phrases and sentences using the vocabulary words.

2. Add some visual appeal. Gather art supplies, photographs, mementos, and other materials to make your poster "pop."

3. Put it all together. Arrange the sentences and phrases from step 1 on the poster and use the materials from step 2 to make the project eye-catching.

4. Share your poster with your family, friends, and classmates.

Master It: Use Words in Meaningful Ways

Have a Conversation

Directions: In this activity, you and your classmates will have a conversation with your teacher. The goal is to use as many vocabulary words as possible during the conversation. Here's how it works:

1. Your teacher will divide the class into teams.

2. Your teacher will get a conversation started by reading one of these prompts:

   > I wonder how our community will be different 25 years from now. Will our school be the same or different? What about the neighborhoods where we live?

   > If an alien from outer space visited our class/school/town, how might this creature react? What might it think? How would *you* react?

3. Raise your hand to signal that you want to share in the conversation. Then state a sentence that uses a vocabulary word *and* that makes sense in the conversation.

4. When one or more conversations are finished, your teacher will add up each team's points and declare a winner.

List 6   Words with Verb Suffixes

Here are four suffixes that form verbs, words that describe action. Note that these suffixes all have the same meaning. Study them and the list of ten words (all verbs) that are formed with them. Read each word, what it means, and how it's used.

Suffix	Meaning	Examples
-ate	to make	acti**vate**, dupli**cate**, evapo**rate**
-en	to make	moist**en**, strength**en**
-fy	to make	magni**fy**, puri**fy**, testi**fy**
-ize	to make	lega**lize**, popular**ize**

Word	What It Means	How It's Used
activate *(v)* AK-tuh-vayt	*to make* active	Pressing this button will *activate* the machine.
duplicate *(v)* DOO-pli-kayt	*to make* a copy of (literally, "to make double")	My teacher used the copy machine to *duplicate* the grammar handout.
evaporate *(v)* i-VAP-uh-rayt	*to make* or change from liquid or solid to vapor	The puddle quickly *evaporated* in the afternoon sun.
moisten *(v)* MOY-suhn	*to make* moist	*Moisten* the sponge so that you can wipe the table.
strengthen *(v)* STRENGK-thuhn	*to make* strong	Exercise will *strengthen* your muscles.
magnify *(v)* MAG-nuh-fie	*to make* great or large (from Latin *magnus*, meaning "great")	This camera lens will *magnify* distant objects.
purify *(v)* PYOOR-uh-fie	*to make* pure	Filters are used to *purify* water.
testify *(v)* TES-tuh-fie	*to make* sworn statements in a court of law	Mr. Jackson will *testify* at the trial of the accused thief.
legalize *(v)* LEE-guh-lahyz	*to make* legal, or permitted by law	Many people believe that it is wrong to *legalize* gambling.
popularize *(v)* POP-yuh-luh-rahyz	*to make* popular	Teenagers helped to *popularize* text messaging.

Own It: Develop Your Word Understanding

Talking in Class

Directions: Work with a partner to complete the activity. Here's what to do:

1. Your teacher will assign you and your partner one word from the vocabulary list above. Do three things:

   (a) Identify the word's suffix and practice saying the word aloud.

   (b) Express the word's meaning in your own words.

   (c) Think of one other word (not in the vocabulary list) that uses the same suffix. Then go to step 2 on the next page.

2. You and your partner present your word to the class. Do three things:

(a) Pronounce the word and then state what the suffix is.

(b) Explain the word's meaning.

(c) Give an example of another word that uses the same suffix.

Link It: Make Word-to-World Connections

It's All in Your Head

Directions: Work with a partner to complete the activity. Here's what to do:

1. Read the headings in the table that follows.

2. Your partner will read each vocabulary word aloud from page 35. After you hear each word, write it in one of the columns.

This word is completely new to me.	I have heard this word before, but I've never used it.	I have used this word before.

3. Repeat step 2. This time, you read the words aloud to your partner.

4. Compare lists. Talk about when you have heard these words before and how you have used them. Read the words in the first column aloud to help them become more familiar.

Master It: Use Words in Meaningful Ways

Give Commands

Directions: The vocabulary words in this list are all action verbs. They are used in sentences to express action. These verbs can also be used in *imperative* sentences, sentences that give commands or orders. Notice how the verbs are used as commands in these examples: "*Activate* the alarm, please." "Do not *duplicate* my test answers." To practice using the vocabulary words to write imperative sentences, follow these steps:

1. Compose a list of related commands. For instance, you could write a set of "Classroom Dos and Don'ts" or "Tips for Becoming Famous." (You can choose whether to make the commands serious or funny.) In your list, try to use at least three different vocabulary words.

2. Pair up with a classmate. Read each other's list and suggest additions to each list.

3. Together, create a third list of related commands. Try to use vocabulary words that you haven't used yet.

List 7   Words with Adjective Suffixes

Now here are four suffixes that form adjectives, words that describe nouns. Study these suffixes and the list of words (adjectives) that contain them. Read each word, what it means, and how it's used.

Suffix	Meaning	Examples
-en	made of or like	gol**den**, silk**en**
-ful	full of or having	doubt**ful**, pain**ful**
-less	without	color**less**, sleep**less**, thought**less**
-ous	full of or having	courage**ous**, graci**ous**, spaci**ous**

Word	What It Means	How It's Used
golden *(adj)* GOHL-duhn	*made of* or like gold	Treasure hunters searched for the *golden* statue.
silken *(adj)* SIL-kuhn	*like* silk	Beth's *silken* hair shone in the sunlight.
doubtful *(adj)* DOUT-fuhl	*having* doubt	Ian was *doubtful* about his chances of making the team.

continued

painful (adj) PAYN-fuhl	*full of* pain	When the couple broke up, it was a *painful* experience for them both.
colorless *(adj)* KUHL-er-lis	*without* color	Water is a *colorless* liquid.
sleepless *(adj)* SLEEP-lis	*without* sleep	Matt spent a *sleepless* night, worrying about what would happen.
thoughtless *(adj)* THAWT-lis	*without* thought	Your *thoughtless* remark hurt my feelings.
courageous *(adj)* kuh-RAY-juhs	*having* courage	Someday, *courageous* space explorers will travel to distant planets.
gracious *(adj)* GRAY-shuhs	*having* grace	We thanked our *gracious* host for welcoming us into her home.
spacious *(adj)* SPAY-shuhs	*full of* space	The *spacious* closet held all of their shoes, jackets, and sports equipment.

Own It: Develop Your Word Understanding

Suffix Matchup

Directions: In this activity, you will be given a suffix *or* a base word. Your job is to find a classmate who has the other half of your word. Here's how the activity works:

1. Your teacher will write each List 7 vocabulary word on an index card, and cut the cards in half so that the base word is on one half, and the suffix is on the other half. Then your teacher will jumble the cards together in a box.

2. Each student chooses one card from the box.

3. Move around the classroom to find the person who has the other half of your word. When you find that person, practice saying the complete word aloud. Write the word (using correct spelling!) on a sheet of paper and review the word's meaning.

4. When everyone has found a word partner, share the results. One of you reads the word aloud to the class. The other person states the word's meaning.

Link It: Make Word-to-World Connections

I'm Thinking of a Word . . .

Directions: In this activity, you and your classmates will use the vocabulary words to describe things in your own lives. Here's how the activity works:

1. Cut two strips of paper. On each one, write the name of something in your life that could be described by one of the vocabulary words on pages 37–38. For instance, you might write *hair* on one slip and *sister* on the other.

2. Your teacher will collect all the slips of paper and jumble them in a box. Then he or she will pull out one slip and read the word aloud.

3. Students suggest one or more vocabulary words that logically describe the word. (If the word is one of *your* two words, stay silent.)

4. Repeat the process with the next slip of paper pulled from the box.

5. *Bonus:* Write word pairs created during this activity to use in the next activity.

Master It: Use Words in Meaningful Ways

Once Upon a Time

Directions: In this activity, you'll use the vocabulary words to write a short story. Follow these steps:

1. Use the vocabulary words on pages 37–38 to brainstorm a list of adjective-noun word pairs. You can use word pairs created in the I'm Thinking of a Word activity, above.

2. Circle the word pairs in your list that could relate to one another. For example, *silken hair* and *courageous sister* could inspire a story about a girl who donates her long hair to a company that makes wigs for cancer survivors.

3. Write a rough draft of your story. It doesn't have to be long. Focus on one event or conversation between characters.

4. Meet with a partner and give feedback on each other's story. Make changes to improve your story.

5. Write the final draft of your story. Host a storytime during lunch with your friends, or read the story aloud to your family.

List 8 Words with Adverb Suffixes

Here is the last list of suffixes in this chapter. These are suffixes that form adverbs, words that describe adjectives or other adverbs. Study these suffixes and the list of words (adverbs) that contain them. Read each word, what it means, and how it's used.

Suffix	Meaning	Examples
-ly	in a certain way	affectionately, conveniently, hurriedly, incredibly, publicly
-ward	in the direction of	downward, skyward, upward
-wise	in the direction of	clockwise, lengthwise

Word	What It Means	How It's Used
affectionately *(adv)* uh-FEK-shuhn-it-lee	with warm, loving feelings (affection)	The puppy *affectionately* licked my hand.
conveniently *(adv)* KUHN-veen-yuhnt-lee	in a way that is easy to use or get to	The post office is *conveniently* located near the center of town.
hurriedly *(adv)* HUR-eed-lee	in a hurry or rush; quickly	Hearing a crash in the kitchen, Mom *hurriedly* came downstairs.
incredibly *(adv)* in-KRED-uh-blee	in a way that is hard to believe	Benjamin is an *incredibly* fast runner.
publicly *(adv)* PUHB-lik-lee	in a public way; openly	The candidate *publicly* apologized for the incorrect statement.
downward *(adv)* DOUN-werd	toward a lower place or position	As the balloon lost air, it drifted slowly *downward*.
skyward *(adv)* SKY-werd	toward the sky	The rocket rose from its launching pad and headed *skyward*.
upward *(adv)* UHP-werd	toward a higher place or position	The hawk flew out of the nest and soared *upward*.
clockwise *(adv)* KLOK-wize	in the direction in which the hands of a clock move	To tighten the screw, turn it *clockwise*.
lengthwise *(adv)* LENGKTH-wize	in the direction of the length	We know the width of this room, but we need to measure it *lengthwise*.

Own It: Develop Your Word Understanding

Suffix Wheels

Directions: Follow the steps to complete the activity.

1. Fill in the three Suffix Wheels that follow by writing the meaning of each word in the space provided.

2. In each empty section of a wheel, write an additional word from the vocabulary list that uses the given suffix, along with the meaning of the word.

3. Your teacher will call out someone's name and identify a suffix. That person reads one of the sections in that Suffix Wheel. Then that person calls out someone else's name and identifies a suffix.

4. Continue calling out names and reading sections from the wheels until each wheel has been read completely.

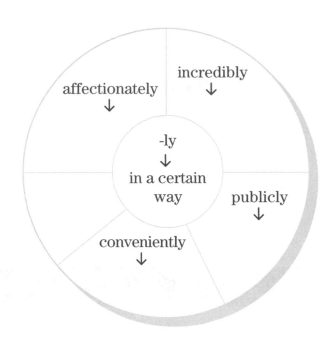

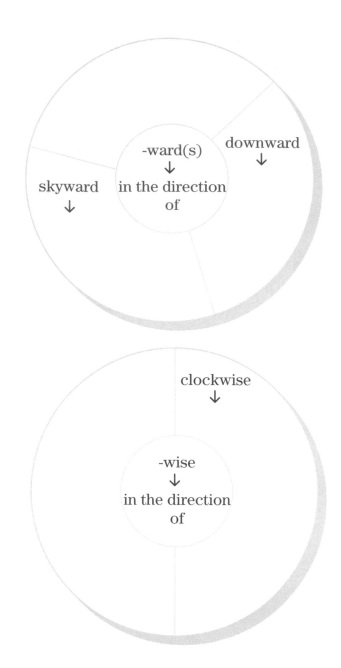

Link It: Make Word-to-World Connections

Let Me Explain

Directions: Can you explain how to perform a dance move using the word *clockwise*? Can you explain how to avoid embarrassing yourself *publicly*? Think about how the vocabulary words relate to something you know how to do. Then follow these steps:

1. Write a few sentences that explain how to do something. You can be serious or funny. You can explain something that your friends know little about, or something that is familiar to many. The goal is to use two or more vocabulary words from List 8 (page 40) in your explanation.

2. Gather in small groups. Read your explanation aloud. Then ask group members to identify the vocabulary words used in your explanation. Ask them if they can suggest yet another vocabulary word that would fit in your explanation.

Master It: Use Words in Meaningful Ways

Adverb Seeks Adjective

Directions: An *adverb* can be used to modify (describe) an *adjective* in a sentence. Here's an example: When I heard her excuse, I was *incredibly angry*. (*Incredibly* is the adverb describing the adjective *angry*. The speaker wasn't just angry, but *incredibly* so.)

   With a partner, play around with the adverbs and adjectives in the vocabulary lists on pages 37–38 and 40. See how many adverb-adjective pairs you can use in sentences. Read your best sentence aloud to the class.

Wrapping Up: Review What You've Learned

Here's a brief summary of what you've studied in this chapter.

> A **suffix** is a group of letters added to the end of a base word or root so as to change its meaning or create a new word. Many words have more than one suffix.

> Every suffix has its own meaning. Adding different suffixes to the same base word creates new words with different meanings and uses.

> A suffix may have more than one meaning. Two different suffixes can have the same meaning.

> Some suffixes are spelled in more than one way.

> Knowing the meaning of a suffix will help you identify a word's part of speech and see how the word relates to other words in the sentence.

> You've learned the following suffixes and their meanings, and words that are formed with them.

-ant, -ent (person or thing that)	-en (to make)
-dom (state or condition)	-fy (to make)
-er, -or (person who)	-ize (to make)
-ment (condition of being, or action, process, or result)	-en (made of or like)
	-ful (full of or having)
-ate (to make)	-less (without)
-ous (full of or having)	-ward (in the direction of)
-ly (in a certain way)	-wise (in the direction of)

Chapter Review Exercises

 Flaunt It: Show Your Word Understanding

In the following exercises, you'll demonstrate your understanding of each vocabulary word. You will use vocabulary words, or forms of the words, to complete sentences and to write sentences of your own.

A Matching

Directions: Match the underlined word to its definition. Write the letter of the definition on the line provided.

_____ **1.** Ryan stared at the velvet bag, tied with <u>silken</u> cord, and wondered what it contained.

_____ **2.** After the play was over, the director <u>publicly</u> thanked the stagehands for building the beautiful set.

_____ **3.** My grandmother hugged me <u>affectionately</u> and thanked me for having visited her.

_____ **4.** Let's go around the circle <u>clockwise</u> and introduce ourselves.

_____ **5.** The thorn in the lion's paw must have been <u>painful</u>.

_____ **6.** When the sergeant heard the sound of a helicopter, he looked <u>skyward</u>.

_____ **7.** To make a paper airplane, first fold a sheet of paper <u>lengthwise</u>.

_____ **8.** If you want fireworks <u>legalized</u> within the city limits, then sign this petition.

_____ **9.** Harry Potter <u>popularized</u> round eyeglasses.

_____ **10.** The container was made from a <u>colorless</u> plastic, allowing its contents to be visible.

a. with warmth and love

b. in the direction in which the hands of a clock move

c. without color

d. to make popular

e. like silk

f. in the direction of the length

g. toward the sky

h. to make legal

i. full of pain

j. in a public way; openly

B Sentence Completion

Directions: Circle the letter of the word that best completes each sentence.

11. The Fourth of July is a holiday set aside to celebrate _____.

    a. boredom   **b.** freedom

    c. amazement   **d.** judgment

12. Alexis flipped a switch on the control pad to _____ the electronic race car.

    a. activate   **b.** evaporate

    c. magnify   **d.** testify

13. For a shy person, entering a talent show is a _____ thing to do.

    a. doubtful   **b.** thoughtless

    c. courageous   **d.** gracious

14. In the cafeteria I spilled hot sauce on my shirt, but _____, I have a spare shirt in my gym locker.

    a. conveniently   **b.** incredibly

    c. graciously   **d.** affectionately

15. Is it true that boiling water from a creek will _____ it, making it safe to drink?

    a. duplicate   **b.** moisten

    c. strengthen   **d.** purify

C Writing

Directions: Follow the directions to write sentences using vocabulary words. Write your sentences on a separate sheet of paper.

16. Use *sleepless* to tell something about yourself.

17. Use *golden* in a description of something in nature.

18. Use *narrator* and *inhabitant* in the same sentence.

19. Use *encouragement* and *manager* in the same sentence.

20. Use *immigrant* and *resident* in the same sentence.

Activities à la Carte: Extend Your Word Knowledge

The activities on this page are presented à la carte, like items on a restaurant menu, meaning that you can choose from a variety of options. Your teacher may assign an activity or let you pick the one that tempts your appetite. If time allows, you might do more than one activity. All of the activities feature the same ingredient: **suffixes**. Dig in!

Caution: Suffixes at Work

Grab your favorite fashion magazine, sports pages, graphic novel, or textbook—and then do your homework! Read the first paragraph or two (or page or two in a graphic novel). Make a list of each word you find that uses a suffix. Then make a master list of the suffixes used. Share the results with your class and explain the importance of the suffixes in the passage. (For instance, could the passage be written *without* the suffixes?)

Mirror, Mirror

In this chapter, you studied **noun** suffixes, **verb** suffixes, **adjective** suffixes, and **adverb** suffixes. Which type best reflects your personality? Do you, like verb suffixes, bring action wherever you go? Or do you see the beauty in details, like adjective suffixes? Write a paragraph explaining what kind of suffix you are most like and why.

 ## In Other Words

Do you speak a language other than English? Get out the short story you wrote for the activity on page 39. Translate the story into that language. What happens to the suffixes in words when you translate them? Do the translated words contain suffixes? Do the suffixes in the second language sound similar to the English versions? Share your translated story with someone who speaks the language.

A Golden Tongue

Use suffixes to increase your persuasive powers. Do you want your mom to haul you and your loud, smelly friends to the beach? Talk to her about the *silken* sand, a *golden* tan, and an *environment* that banishes *boredom*. Identify something you need someone else's help with and use suffixes to write a persuasive appeal. Deliver the request and see what happens.

Say It in 3-D

Sometimes, a lesson in suffixes can seem . . .*flat*. Pump up the lesson to 3-D and add some fun. Create a poster that teaches suffixes (what they are, what some of them mean, etc.). On the poster, use anything *but* flat media. Use Scrabble tiles instead of ink. Use bubble paint, or trace words in glue and sprinkle on glitter. Use collage, toothpicks, Styrofoam—you get the idea. Share your creation with the class.

In the News

Do you have access to a video recorder or a camera? Create a news story about suffixes in your community. Working with a partner, film short segments in which you stand before a store sign, poster, or other printed item and report on the presence (or absence) of suffixes. If you are using a camera, photograph the signs and use the photographs in a "live" broadcast to your class.

Testing, Testing

Use your knowledge of suffixes to create five "fake" words that sound as if they *might* be real. Examples are *actify* (the real word is *activate*) and *residor* (the real word is *resident*). Choose five real words that use suffixes and make a list including the real and fake words in no particular order. Show the list to family members and friends, asking them to sort real from fake. Which of your fake words pass for real? Report to your class.

Learning Words Through Roots

3

Objectives

In this chapter, you will learn

> What a root is

> Why you should know roots

> Words with Greek and Latin roots

How often have you sat through movie previews, waiting for the main attraction? Sure, you're interested in the previews, and they may have something in common with the main attraction. You may even decide to go see one of those movies. But really, you're there to see the main attraction.

You can think of Chapters 1 and 2 as previews for this chapter. In those chapters, you learned a lot about prefixes, suffixes, and using these parts to build words. During those lessons, however, you kept hearing about **roots** and **base words**. No matter how useful a prefix or suffix is, it cannot carry complete meaning without a root or base. For example, you wouldn't use *re-* alone in a sentence, but you would use *report*. With that in mind, in this chapter you'll study the main attraction: roots and base words.

Sneak Peek: Preview the Lesson

Digging Up Roots

The following table contains vocabulary words from this lesson. Think of these words as colorful blossoms with roots hidden beneath the ground. In this activity, your job is to dig up the roots and look at them. How? By looking up each word in a dictionary.

In the dictionary entry for each word, look for a section called *etymology* or *origin*. This section will name one or more languages that are the origins of the word. List these languages in the Origin column. Then answer the questions at the bottom of the table.

Tip: Besides a dictionary, you can consult an etymology dictionary such as the Online Etymology Dictionary Web site.

Key Word	Origin
microscope	
portable	
biography	
archaeology	
expose	

Question Based on Your Findings Above

Can a word's history include more than one language? _____
Think about why your answer to the question above is true.

Vocabulary Mini-Lesson: All About Roots

A **root** is the main word part that you can build different words on. A root is different from a base word. A base word is a complete word and can stand alone. A root usually cannot stand alone as a word.

In Chapters 1 and 2, you saw examples of roots combined with prefixes and suffixes. What are the roots in the following words? What kind of word part is added to each root?

re- + *port* = report (literally, "to carry back")
                 (carry)

re- + *ject* = reject (literally, "to throw back")
                 (throw)

clar   +   *-(i)fy*   =   clarify ("to make clear")
(clear)

cert   +   *-(i)fy*   =   certify ("to make sure or certain")
(sure)

Why Learn This?

Like prefixes and suffixes, roots come from other languages, such
as Greek and Latin. Knowing some common Greek and Latin
roots will help you figure out the meanings of new words. In fact,
some roots will help you understand a wide range of words in the
same large "family." For example, the Latin root *vid* or *vis* means
"to see." Here are just *some* of the many words built on that root.

Vid, Vis Word Family

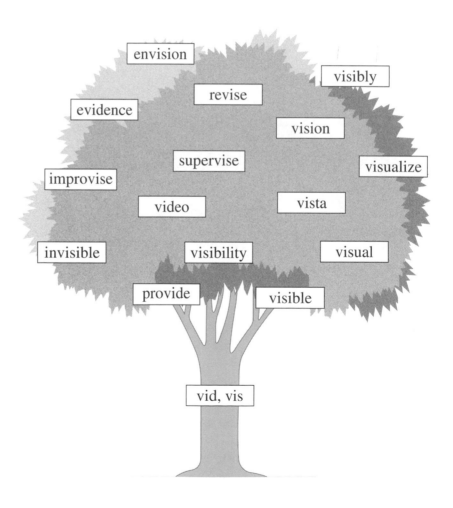

How does each word in this word family involve "seeing"? Check
a dictionary if you're not sure. Can you suggest any words to add?

> ## Tip
>
> It's not always easy to figure out how the different parts of a word give the word its meaning. Sometimes you have to think about it creatively. For example, in Chapter 2 (page 35), you saw that *magnify* (*magni* + *-fy*) literally means "to make great." In what way does a *magnifying* glass make an object "great"?

Prefixes, roots, and suffixes are often called the building blocks of words. By combining your knowledge of prefixes, roots, and suffixes, you'll be able to figure out many words by breaking them down into their parts. What parts make up the following words?

PREFIX	+	ROOT	+	SUFFIX	=	WORD
in- (not)	+	*vis* (see)	+	*-ible* (able to be)	=	invisible (not able to be seen)
re- (back)	+	*port* (carry)	+	*-er* (person who)	=	reporter (person who "carries back" information)
pro- (forward)	+	*ject* (throw)	+	*-or* (thing that)	=	projector (machine that "throws forward" images)

Words to Know: Vocabulary Lists and Activities

Greek and Latin have contributed thousands of words that have become part of the English language. In the word lists you're about to study, you will see many examples of words built on Greek and Latin roots.

Here are a few important points to remember.

> A root may have only one meaning (*port* means "carry," as in *report* and *transport*), or it may have more than one.

For example, the Latin root *ten* can mean either "stretch" as in *extend, tension,* and *tendon,* or "hold," as in *tenant.*

> Two different roots can have the same meaning. For instance, the Latin roots *vis* and *spect* and the Greek root *scope* all mean "see":

vis: vision, visible

spect: spectacle, spectator

scope: telescope, kaleidoscope

> Some roots are spelled in more than one way. For example, the Latin root *mit* means "send," as in *transmit* and *permit.* The root is also spelled *miss,* as in *dismiss* and *mission.*

List 9 Words with Greek Roots

Here are four common Greek roots. Study these roots and the list of ten words that contain them. Read each word, what it means, and how it's used.

Root	Meaning	Examples
graph	write	biography, photograph, seismograph
logy	the study of or science of	archaeology, geology, zoology
meter	measure	barometer, kilometer
scope	see or view	microscope, periscope

Word	What It Means	How It's Used
biography *(n)* bye-OG-ruh-fee	a written account of a person's life (*bio* comes from the Greek word *bios*, meaning "life")	After researching Abraham Lincoln's life, the author wrote a detailed *biography*.
photograph *(n)* FOH-tuh-graf	a picture taken with a camera (*photo* comes from the Greek word for "light")	Kevin recognized the mayor from her *photograph* in the newspaper.
seismograph *(n)* SIZE-muh-graf	an instrument for recording how strong an earthquake is and how long it goes on (*seismo* comes from *seismos*, Greek for "earthquake")	Based on *seismograph* readings, scientists knew that the earthquake had been extremely powerful.

continued

archaeology *(n)* ahr-kee-OL-uh-jee	the scientific study of past life and culture (*archaeo* comes from the Greek word *archaios,* meaning "ancient")	Jessica's interest in ancient cities led her to study *archaeology* in college.
geology *(n)* jee-OL-uh-jee	the scientific study of the earth (*geo* comes from the Greek word for "earth")	An expert in *geology* spoke to our class about rocks and minerals.
zoology *(n)* zoh-OL-uh-jee	the scientific study of animals (*zoo* comes from a Greek word meaning "animal")	After getting her degree in *zoology,* Samantha found a job at the National Zoo in Washington, D.C.
barometer *(n)* buh-ROM-i-ter	instrument for measuring the pressure of the atmosphere (*baro* comes from *baros,* Greek for "weight")	The rising *barometer* reading suggests that tomorrow's weather will be dry and cold.
kilometer *(n)* kil-OM-i-ter	a unit of length equal to 1000 meters	My house is three *kilometers* from school.
microscope *(n)* MY-kruh-skohp	an instrument for making tiny objects appear larger (the Greek prefix *micro-* means "small")	Medical students use *microscopes* to study blood cells.
periscope *(n)* PER-uh-skohp	an instrument for seeing objects that are outside the viewer's direct line of sight (the Greek prefix *peri-* means "around")	The submarine's *periscope* extended above the water.

Own It: Develop Your Word Understanding

Chunk It!

Directions: In this activity, you'll break vocabulary words into parts, or chunks. Then you'll show the class how to put the words back together. Follow these steps:

1. Your teacher will place you in groups of three and assign your group a Greek root (*graph, logy, meter,* or *scope*). Then do two things:

    (a) Study the vocabulary words that use your root. Practice saying the words aloud and discuss each word's meaning.

    (b) On an index card, write the root in large letters. On other cards, write the other chunks that help form each vocabulary word (one word chunk per card).

2. Now it's time to present your words to the class. For each word, do two things:

   (a) One of you stands in front of the class and holds up the root. Tell what the root means.

   (b) Next, one of you stands next to the "root," holding up another card to form a complete word. (It will take three of you to present *biography*.) Say the word aloud and tell what it means.

Link It: Make Word-to-World Connections

Have You Ever . . .

Directions: In this activity, you will tell your classmates how you have used, read about, or heard about one of the vocabulary words from List 9. Here's how the activity works:

1. Your teacher will begin by asking a student, "Have you ever used a *microscope*?"

2. That student answers yes or no. If yes, tell something about how you used the microscope. If no, tell how or why you *think* a microscope would be used. Then choose a different vocabulary word and use it in a question to another student.

3. That student answers your question, then asks someone else a question, and so on.

Master It: Use Words in Meaningful Ways

Hands On

Directions: Each word in List 9 is a noun. Which of these nouns name something that is unfamiliar to you? To learn more about one of these things or ideas, follow these steps:

1. Investigate the thing or idea named by the noun. For instance, look up the word in an encyclopedia, find a book about the idea, interview a knowledgeable person, or find and use the thing.

2. Write a summary of what you learned. In your summary, tell what noun (vocabulary word) you investigated and what you found out. If possible, draw, print out, or cut out a picture of the object, or find an image that represents the idea.

3. Your teacher will collect everyone's summaries and pictures and sort them into folders—one folder per vocabulary word. Whenever you have a few free minutes in class, read some of the summaries that your classmates composed.

List 10   Words with Latin Roots

Now study these Latin roots and ten words that are formed with them. Read each word, what it means, and how it's used.

Root	Meaning	Examples
ped	foot	**ped**estal, **ped**estrian, **ped**ometer
pon, pos	put or place	ex**pos**e, im**pos**e, op**pon**ent
port	carry	ex**port**, **port**able
scrib, script	write	in**scrib**e, manu**script**

Word	What It Means	How It's Used
pedestal (n) PED-uh-stl	a base supporting a column; also, a stand for displaying a statue or sculpture	The museum places many of its sculptures on stone *pedestals*.
pedestrian (n) puh-DES-tree-uhn	a person traveling on foot	*Pedestrians* should look both ways before crossing the street.
pedometer (n) puh-DOM-i-ter	an instrument that records the distance a person walks	According to the *pedometer* clipped to his sneaker, Zach had run two miles.
expose (v) ik-SPOZE	to make known; reveal	The newspaper article *exposed* the truth about the senator.
impose (v) im-POZE	to push or force into being; to push into the notice or company of someone	I don't mean to *impose* on you, but do you mind if I stay for dinner?
opponent (n) uh-POH-nuhnt	a person who goes against another, as in a game or contest (literally, "person who is placed against")	Gabrielle defeated her *opponent* in the chess match.
export (v) ik-SPAWRT	to carry or send to another country	China *exports* many products to the United States.
portable (adj) PAWR-tuh-buhl	that can be carried or easily moved	A *portable* television set is usually not very heavy.

continued

inscribe *(v)* in-SKRAHYB	to write or engrave (cut or carve)	Mr. Patel asked the jeweler to *inscribe* "To my wife, with love" on the silver bracelet.
manuscript *(n)* MAN-yuh-skript	handwritten or typewritten document (literally, "written by hand")	The editor corrected several errors in the author's *manuscript*.

Own It: Develop Your Word Understanding

Draw It!

Directions: In this activity, you will *draw* simple sketches to help yourself recall the meaning of each List 10 vocabulary word. Follow these steps:

1. Study the list of vocabulary words and definitions.

2. Write a different vocabulary word in each box in the organizer. Practice saying the word aloud.

3. Draw a simple picture that will help you remember the meaning of each word. For example, to remember *export*, you might draw a box labeled Products. Beneath the box, write, "From the United States to China."

4. When you have finished filling in the table, share your work with a classmate for further ideas and inspiration. Make any changes that you discover are needed.

My Memory Cues	
Word: Sketch	Word: Sketch
Word: Sketch	Word: Sketch

continued

My Memory Cues	
Word: Sketch	Word: Sketch
Word: Sketch	Word: Sketch
Word: Sketch	Word: Sketch

Link It: Make Word-to-World Connections

Apples and Oranges

Directions: In this activity, you'll work with a partner to group the vocabulary words into categories. Here's what to do:

1. Review the vocabulary words and their meanings (pages 56–57). Do some of the words seem connected in meaning or in how they are used? For instance, do some words relate to a common activity, object, or idea?

2. Identify two or three categories for grouping the vocabulary words. Write these categories in the organizer that follows.

3. Write the vocabulary words in the organizer beneath the relevant category. If a word doesn't fit in any category, write it under "unrelated words." You can write a word in more than one category.

Category 1	Category 2	Category 3	Unrelated words
_____	_____	_____	

> We have a soccer game against our rival school this weekend. Our <u>opponent</u> crushed us the last time, so this time we need to <u>expose</u> their weak defense and <u>impose</u> our superior offense.

Master It: Use Words in Meaningful Ways

Class Mag

Directions: In this activity, you'll help create a magazine that showcases vocabulary words with Latin roots. Working with a partner, follow these steps:

1. Your teacher will assign a vocabulary word to you (or let you choose one). Your job is to create one magazine page that showcases this word. Here are some ideas:

   > create an advertisement

   > write and illustrate an article

> write and illustrate a short story, poem, or skit
> create a word game
> write an advice column

2. To create your magazine page, use neatly written or printed text, your own artwork, magazine cutouts, or other materials. Be sure that your page uses the vocabulary word and makes its meaning clear!

3. Your teacher will assemble everyone's page into a finished magazine by using a folder with brads, staples, or another method. The magazine will be available for you to read when you have spare time.

Wrapping Up: Review What You've Learned

Here's a brief summary of what you've studied in this chapter.

> A **root** is a word part from which other words are formed. A root differs from a base word. A base word can stand alone, while a root usually cannot.

> Like prefixes and suffixes, roots also come from other languages, such as Greek and Latin.

> A root may have just one meaning, or it may have more than one.

> Two different roots can have the same meaning.

> Some roots are spelled in more than one way.

> Learning roots will help you understand the meanings of words built on those roots.

> You learned the following roots and words that are formed with them.

graph (write)	ped (foot)
logy (the science or study of)	pon, pos (put or place)
meter (measure)	port (carry)
scope (see or view)	scrib, script (write)

Flaunt It: Show Your Word Understanding

In the following exercises, you'll demonstrate your understanding of each vocabulary word. You will use vocabulary words, or forms of the words, to complete sentences and to write sentences of your own.

A Sentence Completion

Directions: Circle the letter of the word that best completes each sentence.

1. Through my study of _____, I learned to recognize igneous, sedimentary, and metamorphic rocks.

    a. seismographs   **b.** geology
    c. zoology   **d.** pedestals

2. As a special project, my gym teacher lent me a _____ to use for a day.

    a. barometer   **b.** kilometer
    c. pedometer   **d.** periscope

3. This _____ should make it easier for you to study the wings of the housefly.

    a. microscope   **b.** pedestrian
    c. manuscript   **d.** archaeology

4. To find out why Lincoln decided to run for the presidency, consult this _____.

    a. biography   **b.** inscribe
    c. photograph   **d.** opponent

5. I will never forgive you for _____ my secrets to the entire class!

    a. imposing   **b.** portable
    c. exposing   **d.** exporting

B Word Choice

Directions: Underline the word that best completes each sentence.

6. The beach is two (*barometers*, *kilometers*) away. Would you rather walk or ride the bus?

7. As a (*pedestal*, *pedestrian*), you should look both ways before crossing a street.

8. Hiding in an underground cave, the soldier used a (*periscope, microscope*) to search for enemies aboveground.

9. I used a stick to (*inscribe, impose*) my initials in the wet cement.

10. Immediately after the earthquake, scientists consulted (*seismographs, pedometers*) to learn exactly how strong it had been.

(Writing

Directions: Write one or more sentences to answer each of the following questions. Be sure to use the italicized vocabulary word in your sentence. Write your sentences on a separate sheet of paper.

11. If you wrote a *biography* of your best friend, what event would you be sure to include?

12. Where in the world would you enjoy having your *photograph* taken?

13. For a hands-on lesson in *archaeology*, would you rather study a pyramid or a buried city?

14. For a hands-on lesson in *geology*, would you rather go to the Grand Canyon or to a Hawaiian island?

15. For a lesson in *zoology*, would you rather study the habits of a wild animal or a tame animal?

Chapter Extension Activities

Activities à la Carte: Extend Your Word Knowledge

The activities on this page are presented à la carte, like items on a restaurant menu, meaning that you can choose from a variety of options. Your teacher may assign an activity or let you pick the one that tempts your appetite. If time allows, you might do more than one activity. All of the activities feature the same ingredient: **roots**. Dig in!

Your Roots Are Showing

Roots is a multiple-meaning word. That is, it has several different definitions, depending on how it is used. Make a poster or computer presentation to teach your classmates the different uses of *roots*. Be sure to use visuals, along with words, to get your ideas across.

A Rocky Job

Does studying the walls of the Grand Canyon sound like fun? How about digging up an ancient ruin? Perhaps you are a future geologist or archaeologist. Each word in the list of words with Greek roots (page 53) relates to a professional career of some kind. Choose one of these words and find out what a related career would be like. Then report back to your class.

Movie Pitch

Use vocabulary words in this chapter to inspire ideas for a movie. Alone or with a partner, write a plot summary to tell what your movie is about. Write a list of characters with brief descriptions of each. Finally, pitch your movie idea to the class. Ask for a show of hands indicating who would go see your movie.

 ### Repeat After Me

Prepare a minilanguage lesson to teach your classmates a few words in a language other than English. Focus on words that use Greek or Latin roots, like those in this chapter. Explain the meaning of each foreign word and help students with pronunciation. Who knows, maybe you'll teach languages for a living one day!

That's So You!

Create your own personal slogan using at least one word with a Greek or Latin root. Think of a phrase or sentence that expresses your personality, an attitude, a dream, or something else that sums up part of who you are. Then design a poster to display your slogan—something that you could hang on your door or over your bed.

We Are Family

Find a word family living in your home. Choose a Greek or Latin root and list the vocabulary words—plus additional words that you identify—that use this root. Then go word hunting in your home. How many objects can you relate to a word in your list? Is your television an *export* from Korea? Do you have a book *report* on your desk? Use phrases or sentences to make a list of everything you find relating to the word family. Amaze your classmates with the results.

Forming Words with Prefixes and Suffixes

4

Picture this: You are dressed in a football uniform. Now, change the image in your head: You are dressed in fancy clothes. Now, change the image again: You are dressed for the beach.

Each of these images has one thing in common—you yourself form the foundation for each image. However, details are changed to create different effects.

In the same way, you can take a base word or root and "dress it up" with prefixes and suffixes to create different effects, or meanings. Much of the word's meaning depends on the base or root; however, the prefix and/or suffix determines the meaning of the complete word. *Misread* is different from *readable*, and *unreadable* is different from *readability*. A word's meaning depends on its parts.

You can also think of prefixes, roots, and suffixes as the building blocks of words. In this chapter, we'll take a closer look at how these building blocks are combined.

Sneak Peek: Preview the Lesson

Skim and Scan

As you may know, you can determine what a chapter is about by skimming and scanning it. To **skim** a chapter, you run your eyes over the headings, tables, and other features to get an idea of what the chapter is about. To **scan** a chapter, you run your eyes over headings and paragraphs, looking for particular words or ideas.

Skimming and scanning are useful because they allow you to get helpful information quickly.

1. What can you find out by skimming this chapter? Skim the headings, tables, and any other features that stand out. Then write a few phrases or sentences identifying what topics you think the chapter will cover.

_____

_____

_____

2. Scan the chapter for key words such as *prefix*, *suffix*, *root*, and *base*. Based on your scan, what do you expect the chapter to teach you?

_____

_____

_____

Vocabulary Mini-Lesson: How to Add Prefixes and Suffixes

It's usually easy to add a prefix to a word. Just keep all the letters of both the prefix and the base word and put them together.

Study the examples below, which use some of the prefixes you learned in Chapter 1. Notice that no letters are left out or changed.

PREFIX	+	BASE WORD	=	NEW WORD
mis-	+	spell	=	misspell
un-	+	natural	=	unnatural
re-	+	organize	=	reorganize
under-	+	rate	=	underrate
in-	+	complete	=	incomplete

Do you see that no letters are changed or dropped? Even when the last letter of the prefix is the same as the first letter of the base word, keep both letters. For example, adding mis- to spell gives you mi**ss**pell.

Spelling Tip

The prefix *in-*, meaning "not or the opposite of," changes its spelling to *im-* when it's added to a word than starts with *p*:

impatient   impolite   impossible   impure

Now that you've learned how to add prefixes, let's explore how to add suffixes. When you add a suffix to the end of the word, you *usually* keep all the letters of both the suffix and the word, and you do not drop, change, or add any letters. Look at the following examples.

BASE WORD	+	SUFFIX	=	NEW WORD
entertain	+	-ment	=	entertainment
assist	+	-ant	=	assistant
ski	+	-er	=	skier
weak	+	-en	=	weaken
wood	+	-en	=	wooden
delight	+	-ful	=	delightful
fear	+	-less	=	fearless
fortunate	+	-ly	=	fortunately

In forming these words, there are no letters changed or omitted.

However, sometimes adding a suffix *does* affect the spelling of a word. This usually happens when you add suffixes to words ending in *y*, and when you add suffixes to words ending in silent *e*. Let's look at both of these cases.

Adding Suffixes to Words That End in Y

When it comes to attaching suffixes, words ending in *y* can be tricky. That's because not all *y*-ending words follow the same rule. The key is to look at the letter *before* the *y*.

> If the letter before the *y* is a *consonant*, change the *y* to *i* before adding the suffix.

BASE WORD	+	SUFFIX	=	NEW WORD
fancy	+	-ful	=	fanciful
pity	+	-less	=	pitiless
fury	+	-ous	=	furious
sympathy	+	-ize	=	sympathize
clumsy	+	-ly	=	clumsily

Note: There are a few exceptions to this rule, such as *shyness, shyly, dryness, and slyly.*

> If the letter before the *y* is a *vowel*, do *not* change the *y* to *i* before adding the suffix.

BASE WORD	+	SUFFIX	=	NEW WORD
play	+	-ful	=	playful
buy	+	-er	=	buyer

key	+	-less	=	keyless
pay	+	-ment	=	payment
joy	+	-ous	=	joyous

Note: One exception to this rule is *daily* (day + -ly).

Adding Suffixes to Words That End with a Silent *E*

Many words end in a "silent" *e*. This means that the *e* is not pronounced, as in *flame* and *dive*. To figure out how to attach suffixes to words ending with a silent *e*, look at the first letter of the suffix.

> If the suffix starts with a *vowel*, drop the silent *e*.

BASE WORD	+	SUFFIX	=	NEW WORD
serve	+	-ant	=	servant
investigate	+	-or	=	investigator
active	+	-ate	=	activate
adventure	+	-ous	=	adventurous
love	+	-able	=	lovable
believe	+	-able	=	believable

Exceptions: Words ending in *ge* such as *courageous* and *outrageous* keep the silent *e*. Also, words ending in *able* sometimes keep the *e*. Examples: *agreeable, knowledgeable, changeable, manageable, noticeable,* and *rechargeable.*

> If the suffix starts with a *consonant*, keep the silent *e*.

BASE WORD	+	SUFFIX	=	NEW WORD
amuse	+	-ment	=	amusement
wire	+	-less	=	wireless
grace	+	-ful	=	graceful
secure	+	-ly	=	securely

Exceptions: judgment, argument, truly

> However, when you change an adjective ending in *le* to an adverb ending in *ly*, you drop the silent *e*:

ADJECTIVE	+	SUFFIX	=	ADVERB
terrible	+	-ly	=	terribly
simple	+	-ly	=	simply
probable	+	-ly	=	probably
gentle	+	-ly	=	gently

Why Learn This?

Learning to add prefixes and suffixes to words is a great way to expand your vocabulary. When you add word parts, you can create new words with different meanings. For example, when you add *-less* and *-ly* to *fear*, you've created a new word (*fearlessly*) with a very different meaning from the original word, *fear*.

Adding a suffix changes not only a word's meaning but also its part of speech, which lets you use the word for a different purpose. For example, in the phrase, "The firefighter was *fearless*," *fearless* (adjective) describes the firefighter (noun). But when you add another suffix, *-ly*, and change *fearless* to an adverb, *fearlessly*, you can now describe an *action*: The firefighter ran *fearlessly* into the burning building (*fearlessly* describes the verb *ran*, how he ran). The more parts you learn, the more words you can understand and use in different ways.

Words to Know: Vocabulary Lists and Activities

Now that you've learned about adding prefixes and suffixes, you're ready to study some new words that contain these parts.

List 11   Words with Multiple Parts

Here are ten words that contain multiple parts. The letters in dark type are prefixes and suffixes that you learned in Chapters 1 and 2. Read each word, what it means, and how it's used.

Word	What It Means	How It's Used
automatica**lly** *(adv)* aw-tuh-MAT-ik-lee	by itself	The door opens *automatically* as shoppers enter the store.
content**ment** *(n)* kuhn-TENT-muhnt	condition of being content; satisfaction	Dylan had a feeling of *contentment* after he accomplished his goals.
export**er** *(n)* EK-spawrt-er	a country that sells goods to another country (*Note:* You studied the root *port* in Chapter 3, page 56.)	Venezuela is an *exporter* of oil.

continued

inconsiderately (adv) in-kuhn-SID-er-it-lee	without consideration for others; thoughtlessly	Gina acted *inconsiderately* when she practiced her drums at midnight.
internationally (adv) in-ter-NASH-uh-nl-ee	among nations; worldwide	The author is known *internationally*, and her books have sold millions of copies.
miscommunication (n) mis-kuh-MYOO-ni-kayh-shun	unclear or incorrect communication	Speak clearly and listen carefully to prevent *miscommunication*.
misstatement (n) mis-STEYT-muhnt	incorrect statement	The candidate's *misstatement* of the facts confused voters.
misunderstand (v) mis-uhn-der-STAND	to understand incorrectly; get the wrong idea	Did you really say the dog ate your homework, or did I *misunderstand* you?
mysteriously (adv) mi-STEER-ee-uhs-lee	in a way that is difficult to understand or explain	The small stone statue *mysteriously* disappeared from my garden.
proponent (n) pruh-POH-nuhnt	someone who argues in favor of something; supporter (*Note:* You studied the root *pon* in Chapter 3, page 56.)	Mrs. Schuyler is a leading *proponent* of women's rights.

Own It: Develop Your Word Understanding

Exploring Key Words

Directions: Work with a partner to complete the activity. Each of you completes five of the ten graphic organizers on the next pages. Then share your results. For each graphic organizer, follow these steps:

1. Study the vocabulary word in the top box and review its definition on pages 69–70. Then use your own words and ideas to write a definition in the center box of the organizer.

2. Play around with the word's parts—adding and subtracting them—to create other forms of the word. (For instance, *automatic* is an adjective form of the adverb *automatically*.) Write these words in the first box.

3. In the third box, sketch or write a clue to help you remember the key word's meaning.

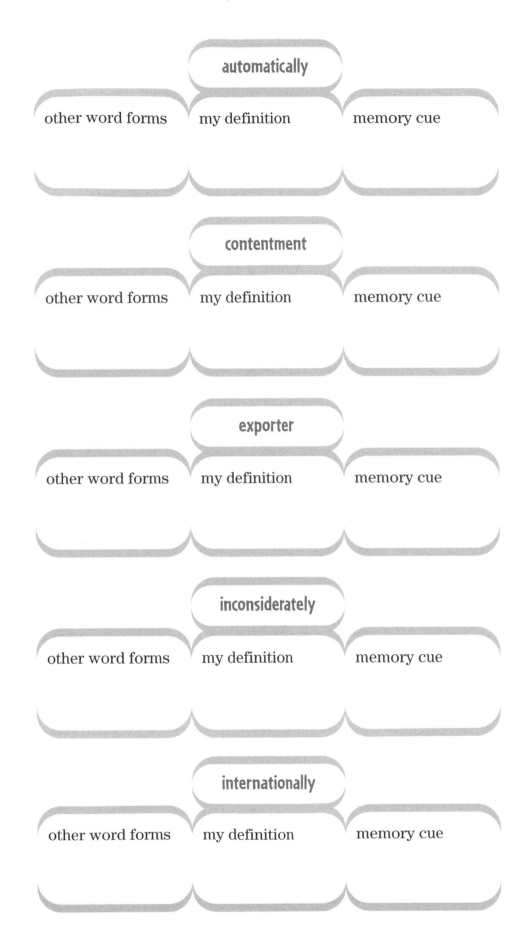

automatically

| other word forms | my definition | memory cue |

contentment

| other word forms | my definition | memory cue |

exporter

| other word forms | my definition | memory cue |

inconsiderately

| other word forms | my definition | memory cue |

internationally

| other word forms | my definition | memory cue |

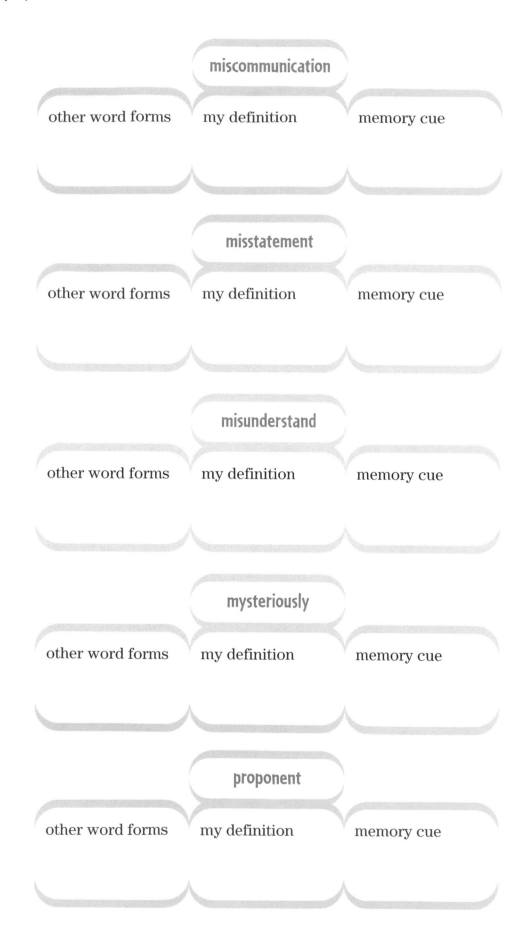

miscommunication

other word forms	my definition	memory cue

misstatement

other word forms	my definition	memory cue

misunderstand

other word forms	my definition	memory cue

mysteriously

other word forms	my definition	memory cue

proponent

other word forms	my definition	memory cue

Link It: Make Word-to-World Connections

Me, Myself, and I

Directions: Follow these steps to complete the activity. Your teacher may ask you to work with a partner.

1. Think about how the key word—or another form of the word—relates to you. For instance, can you use the word to describe yourself? In a comment about a friend? In a description of a dream or favorite activity? In a statement about your community?

2. In the space beside each key word, write a sentence or two telling what the word has to do with you and your world. Be sure to use the key word in your response!

Key Word	What This Word Has to Do with Me
automatically	
contentment	
exporter	
inconsiderately	
internationally	
miscommunication	
misstatement	
misunderstand	
mysteriously	
proponent	

Master It: Use Words in Meaningful Ways

Word Problems

Directions: In a class or small-group discussion, answer each of the following questions. Explain your reasoning.

1. Is a *misstatement* always *inconsiderate*?
2. Can a *proponent* have *mysterious* motivations?
3. Is the *export* business always *international*?
4. When is *contentment automatic*?
5. Does *miscommunication* always cause *misunderstanding*?

List 12   Words with Multiple Parts

Here are ten additional words that contain prefixes and suffixes. Read each word, what it means, and how it's used.

Word	What It Means	How It's Used
reactiv**ate** *(v)* ree-AK-tuh-vayt	to make active again	Workers shut down the machine over the weekend and then *reactivated* it on Monday morning.
reclassi**fy** *(v)* ree-KLAS-uh-fie	to assign to a different category	The document was once considered top secret, but the government has now *reclassified* it.
reform**er** *(n)* ri-FAWR-mer	a person who tries to bring about political or social reform, or improvement	Dorothea Dix was a social *reformer* who worked for better treatment of the mentally ill.
replace**ment** *(n)* ri-PLAYS-muhnt	a person or thing that takes the place of another	When the star quarterback retired, the team had to find a *replacement*.
tear**fully** *(adv)* TEER-fuh-lee	with tears	"I want to go home," my little sister said *tearfully* on the first day of camp.
thought**lessly** *(adv)* THAWT-lis-lee	without thought or consideration for others	You *thoughtlessly* gave away the book I wanted to read.
underpay**ment** *(n)* uhn-der-PAY-muhnt	too little payment	Toni had expected to earn $50 but received only $40, and this *underpayment* upset her.
unevent**ful** *(adj)* uhn-i-VENT-fuhl	without any noteworthy events	Josie didn't have much to say, because it had been an *uneventful* day at school.
ungrac**ious** *(adj)* uhn-GRAY-shuhs	not gracious; rude	It would be *ungracious* for a dinner guest to say he disliked the meal.
unsuccess**fully** *(adv)* uhn-suhk-SES-fuhl-ee	without success	My dad tried *unsuccessfully* to fix the computer.

Own It: Develop Your Word Understanding

Break It Up!

Directions: Work with a partner to complete the activity.

1. Your teacher will assign you a vocabulary word from List 12. Practice saying the word aloud.

2. Break the word up into its parts. You'll have a root word plus one or more prefixes and suffixes. Write each word part on an index card.

3. On the backs of the index cards, write definitions and memory cues for the word parts.

4. Read your key word aloud to the class. Then identify the word parts and tell how they work together to form the key word.

Link It: Make Word-to-World Connections

Have You Ever . . .

Directions: Your teacher will get the activity started by asking a student one of the questions in the box. That person answers by saying yes or no and giving an explanation. Then that person asks someone else a question.

You can use one of the questions below or make up your own question using a vocabulary word.

Have You Ever . . .

. . . *reactivated* a relationship that you previously ended?

. . . *reclassified* your favorite people?

. . . tried to *reform* your ways?

. . . asked for a *replacement* for something?

. . . spoken *tearfully*?

. . . behaved *thoughtlessly*?

. . . felt *underpaid*?

. . . rescued a friend from an *uneventful* day?

. . . felt upset with an *ungracious* person?

. . . laughed at an *unsuccessful* effort?

Master It: Use Words in Meaningful Ways

If You Wrote the News

Directions: Imagine that you are a television news reporter. Your assignment? Attract young viewers by reporting on an interesting topic. Follow these steps:

1. Study the list of vocabulary words (page 75). Think about how some of them relate to a topic of interest to you. (Topic ideas: music, sports, books, movies, hobbies, current events.)

2. Write a 200-word news report on your chosen topic. Use as many vocabulary words (or forms of the words) as possible.

3. Prepare visuals for your report. These may include magazine cutouts, sketches, charts, or photos relating to your news story.

4. Present your report live to the class. *Alternative:* If you have access to the necessary equipment, record your news segment and play it for the class.

Wrapping Up: Review What You've Learned

Here's a brief summary of what you've studied in this chapter.

> In general, to add a prefix to a base word, keep all the letters of both the prefix and the word, even when the last letter of the prefix is the same as the first letter of the word.

> Attaching a suffix to a word is a little trickier than adding a prefix. Most of the time, you keep all the letters of both the suffix and the word and do not drop, change, or add any letters. However, sometimes special rules apply, such as when you add a suffix to a word that ends in *y* or silent *e*.

> To add a suffix to a word that ends in *y*, look at the letter before the *y*. If the letter before the *y* is a consonant, change the *y* to *i* before adding the suffix. If the letter before the *y* is a vowel, do *not* change the *y* to *i* before adding the suffix.

> To add a suffix to a word that ends in a silent *e*, look at the first letter of the suffix. If the suffix starts with a vowel, drop the silent *e* before adding the suffix. If the suffix starts with a consonant, keep the silent *e*. But when changing an adjective ending in *le* to an adverb ending in *ly*, drop the silent *e*.

> Adding prefixes and suffixes to a word can change a word's meaning and change its part of speech.

Flaunt It: Show Your Word Understanding

In the following exercises, you'll demonstrate your understanding of each vocabulary word. You will use vocabulary words, or forms of the words, to complete sentences and to write sentences of your own.

A Matching

Directions: Match each sentence to the word that best completes it. Write the letter of the word on the blank in the sentence. Each word is used only once.

1. W.E.B. DuBois was a social _____ who worked for racial equality.

2. Because of a _____, I thought my curfew was at 8:00 P.M., but really it was at 7:00 P.M.

3. It was _____ of Jordan to grab the first slice of cake at Hannah's birthday party.

4. I have tried _____ to crack this secret code, and now I am asking for your help.

5. If you miss being a part of the online book club, perhaps you would like to _____ your membership.

6. Some U.S. companies are _____ of nuts and nut products, selling items such as nut butters and nut flours overseas.

7. As of Friday, Mr. Jance will no longer be teaching choir. His _____ will be announced tomorrow.

8. This timer will _____ turn on the front porch light at 6:00 P.M. each evening.

9. Did you _____ me when I said not to borrow my clothes without asking?

10. Are you a/an _____ of year-round school, or do you prefer to keep summer vacation?

a. exporters

b. unsuccessfully

c. reformer

d. proponent

e. automatically

f. reactivate

g. ungracious

h. replacement

i. misunderstand

j. miscommunication

 Sentence Completion

Directions: Circle the letter of the word that best completes each sentence.

11. A note from a secret admirer _____ appeared on my desk.

    a. automatically   **b.** thoughtlessly
    c. unsuccessfully   **d.** mysteriously

12. I'm sorry. The _____ was due to an error in math on my part.

    a. underpayment   **b.** proponent
    c. reform   **d.** replacement

13. Last summer Mom canceled our newspaper subscription, but this week she _____ the subscription.

    a. reclassified   **b.** reactivated
    c. exported   **d.** misstated

14. Lying on a towel in the warm sun, I felt _____ with the perfect day.

    a. contentment   **b.** ungracious
    c. misunderstood   **d.** tearful

15. Why is it so easy to treat a brother or sister _____?

    a. internationally   **b.** miscommunication
    c. inconsiderately   **d.** uneventfully

Writing

Directions: Follow the directions to write sentences using vocabulary words, or forms of the words. Write your sentences on a separate sheet of paper.

16. Use *uneventful* to tell about an event that you attended.
17. Use *tearfully* to describe a conversation.
18. Use *contentment* to tell something about yourself.
19. Use *thoughtlessly* to describe a person's behavior.
20. Use *mysteriously* to tell about something that mystifies you.

Chapter Extension Activities

Activities à la Carte: Extend Your Word Knowledge

The activities on this page are presented à la carte, like items on a restaurant menu, meaning that you can choose from a variety of options. Your teacher may assign an activity or let you pick the one that tempts your appetite. If time allows, you might do more than one activity. All of the activities feature the same ingredient: **word parts**. Dig in!

You Crack Me Up

Dust off your funny bone and grab a pencil. Create a single-frame cartoon using a vocabulary word (or form of a word) from this chapter. For instance, use verbal irony—when what the speaker is saying is the opposite of what is actually happening—such as a sketch of a news reporter saying, "Opening day here at the zoo was uneventful," while in the background, a child is opening the door to the monkey cage.

enTITLEment

Collect titles and headlines from books, newspapers, magazines, and other sources. Then analyze the use of word parts in the titles and headlines. Answer such questions as, "Do titles/headlines mostly use words with multiple parts, or more basic words?" and "Does the target audience influence the title's use of words with multiple parts?"

Spare Change

Earn some money by marketing your services as a babysitter, dog walker, yard cleaner, or all-purpose helper. Using new words you've learned, create a flyer. On it, hook clients with a rhetorical question such as, "Have you tried *unsuccessfully* to clean out that garage?" Then sell your service: "Hire me, and in one afternoon I'll *replace* chaos with order." Finally, state your pay rate and contact information.

The Write Stuff

Compete with friends to see who can use word parts in this chapter to create the most new words in five minutes. Open your book to the two lists (pages 69–70 and 75). Then set a timer for five minutes. Create new words and word forms by taking roots and adding different prefixes and suffixes. Then give your new words a reality check—are they real words? Ask your teacher if you can post your list on a class bulletin board.

Time Capsule

Prepare a time capsule that *encapsulates* your life right now. In a shoe box, collect photos, notes from friends, magazine clippings, and other mementos. Also include a letter to yourself summing up your life, your hopes for the future, and other tidbits your future self would like to know. Use vocabulary words from this chapter, or forms of the words, in your letter. Finally, seal the container and affix a note stating when in the future you will open the time capsule.

¡Que Misterioso!

Translate each word in this chapter's word lists into a second language. Is there a direct translation for each word, or must you use a phrase? Can you break the translated word into the same parts as those in the English word? Would you say that one language relies on prefixes and suffixes more than the other language, or do they use these word parts about equally? Share your findings with someone who's interested in languages.

Name Game

With a few friends, play around with using your names as root words. Add prefixes and suffixes, experimenting to create new forms of your name—a verb form, for instance, or an adjective form. Write definitions for your creations. For example, a "Davidment" could mean "a funny comment typical of David." To "Jenniferize" something could mean "to decorate with flowers, as in Jennifer's style."

Learning Words from Other Sources

5

Objectives

In this chapter, you will learn

> How new words come into our language from foreign languages, from mythology, and from the names of people and places

> Common words from some of these various sources

Have you ever borrowed a friend's shirt, cut your hair like a picture in a magazine, or taken a fad and added your own touch? If so, then you know what it means to add to what you have by borrowing from other sources.

Just like you borrow items and ideas, the English language borrows and adapts words from other sources. Some words are borrowed from other languages. Some are based on gods and goddesses in ancient stories, or myths. Some come from the names of people and places. In this chapter, you'll learn a wide range of words from several different sources.

Sneak Peek: Preview the Lesson

Beg, Borrow, or Steal

The following table lists a few of the sources from which the English language borrows words. To become familiar with each type of source, respond to the questions in the second column. *Hint:* You may need to consult a dictionary or other reference source for help with unfamiliar terms.

Sources of Words	Questions for Thought
foreign languages	Name a few foreign languages. Do you ever use a word from one of these languages when you're speaking in English? Explain.
mythology	What are myths? Can you name any characters from myths?
eponyms	What is an eponym?

Vocabulary Mini-Lesson: Words Come from Foreign Languages

These words all have something in common. Can you guess what that is?

cafeteria	coyote	mosquito	potato
canyon	hurricane	patio	ranch

All of these words have been adopted into English from Spanish. Many familiar words come from languages around the world.

Words from foreign languages have been added to English over hundreds of years, and they are still being added today. Over the centuries, whenever English speakers came into contact with people from other cultures through trade, travel, or war, they adopted or "borrowed" some of their words. These words may not seem foreign to us, either because their form and spelling have changed or because we are so used to hearing them.

Did you know, for example, that *kindergarten* is a German word, and *pajamas* comes from Persian? You may be surprised at the origin of some of the words in the following lists.

 **ords to Know: Vocabulary Lists and Activities**

In this section, you'll study two lists of words from a wide variety of languages, including Arabic, French, Spanish, Italian, and Persian.

List 13   Words from Foreign Languages

Here are the first ten words from foreign languages. Read each word, its source, what it means, and how it's used.

Word	Its Source	What It Means	How It's Used
admiral *(n)* AD-mer-uhl	Arabic	the commanding officer of a navy	The sailors stood at attention as the *admiral* boarded the ship.
adobe *(n)* uh-DOH-bee	Spanish	sun-dried brick	Some Native Americans lived in *adobe* houses.
attitude *(n)* AT-i-tood	French	way of acting, thinking, or feeling	Adam shows his serious *attitude* toward school by working hard and getting good grades.
attorney *(n)* uh-TUR-nee	French	a lawyer	The *attorney* tried to persuade the jury that her client was innocent.
ballet *(n)* ba-LAY	French	an artistic form of dance	The *ballet* begins with two dancers twirling across the stage.
banister *(n)* BAN-uh-ster	Italian	a handrail of a staircase	Hold on to the *banister* as you walk down the stairs.
bouquet *(n)* boo-KAY	French	a bunch of flowers	The bride carried an elegant *bouquet* of white roses.
brochure *(n)* broh-SHOOR	French	a pamphlet	The travel *brochure* contains pictures of beautiful beaches.
bronze *(n)* bronz	Italian	a metallic mixture of copper and tin	This sculpture is made of *bronze*.
charity *(n)* CHAR-i-tee	French	the giving of money or service to those in need	The people's *charity* helped to feed the homeless.

Own It: Develop Your Word Understanding

Sensory Appeal

Directions: Study the list of words and their meanings. Then take a moment to let each word come alive in your imagination. How? Think about how each word might appeal to one of the five senses. For instance, *bronze* may appeal to your sense of touch as you imagine how cold and hard a bronze statue would feel.

Write each word and a brief description of its appeal in one of the boxes below.

Sense	How Each Vocabulary Word Appeals to That Sense
sight	
hearing	
taste	
touch	
smell	

Link It: Make Word-to-World Connections

Where in the World?

Directions: Where in *your* world would you most likely encounter the things named by the vocabulary words? With a partner, discuss how you might encounter these people, things, and ideas. Then write each word in one of the boxes below. *Bonus:* Write your own heading in the empty box and add words to this box too.

In a class discussion, explain your categorization of the words.

at home	in a class
out having fun	

Master It: Use Words in Meaningful Ways

Pick Three

Directions: In this activity, you'll help classmates become familiar with three vocabulary words that you know something about. Follow these steps:

  1. Pick three vocabulary words that are familiar or interesting to you. (For ideas, review the two activities previous to this one.)

  2. Write two or three sentences about each of the three words. Do your best to make the meaning of the word clear in the context of what you write. For instance, in using the word *adobe*, you could describe what an adobe brick looks like and how it feels to the touch, or how it compares or contrasts to a brick or cement block.

3. Your teacher will pronounce each vocabulary word aloud. After saying each word, he or she will ask students to read their sentences that tell about that word.

List 14   Words from Foreign Languages

Learn these ten additional words from different languages. Read each word, its source, what it means, and how it's used.

Word	Its Source	What It Means	How It's Used
mammoth *(n)* MAM-uhth	Russian	an extinct mammal of the elephant family	The huge *mammoth* of prehistoric times had long curved tusks.
mirage *(n)* mi-RAHZH	French	an optical illusion in which a person imagines seeing something that isn't there	Travelers saw a *mirage* of a lake in the desert.
safari *(n)* suh-FAHR-ee	Swahili	a journey or hunting expedition	The guide led us on a *safari* through the African jungle.
shawl *(n)* shawl	Persian	a cloth worn as a covering for the head or shoulders	The woman wrapped herself in a colorful *shawl*.
sofa *(n)* SOH-fuh	Arabic	a couch	Courtney sat on the living room *sofa*, reading the newspaper.
souvenir *(n)* soo-vuh-NEER	French	something kept as a reminder	I bought a poster of the Grand Canyon as a *souvenir* of our vacation.
tornado *(n)* tawr-NAY-doh	Spanish	a violently whirling windstorm, usually appearing as a dark, funnel-shaped cloud	The *tornado* destroyed many homes as it moved across the state.
typhoon *(n)* tie-FOON	Chinese	a violent tropical windstorm	Homes near the coast were battered by the *typhoon*.
vague *(adj)* vayg	French	not clear or exact	Instead of a detailed explanation, Tod gave only a *vague* answer.
yacht *(n)* yot	Dutch	a boat for pleasure cruising or racing	The *yacht* bobbed up and down on the waves.

> ### Did You Know?
>
> Just as English has borrowed from other languages, so have other languages borrowed from English. In fact, English words appear in most languages of the world, in either their original or a changed form. Japanese, for example, has its own version of such English words as *computer* (*konpyuta*) and *milk* (*miruku*), while France has borrowed *football*, *drugstore*, and many other English words.

Own It: Develop Your Word Understanding

Think Fast

Directions: In this activity, you'll mingle with classmates—two minutes at a time! Here's what to do:

1. Your teacher will assign you a vocabulary word from List 14. Write it at the top of a sheet of paper. Then grab a pencil, stand up, and get ready to mingle.

2. Your teacher will announce, "Start." You have two minutes to pair up with a classmate and, together, write a logical sentence using both of your vocabulary words.

3. After two minutes, your teacher will call time. Quickly, write the sentence you composed (if you haven't already). If the sentence seems illogical, or you were unable to write a sentence, make a note of that.

4. Now get ready to go again—and pair up with someone different.

5. When the activity is over, hand in your sentences *or* exchange them with a classmate for evaluation, as your teacher directs.

Link It: Make Word-to-World Connections

Now and Later

Directions: In this activity, you'll think about words you're learning now and how these words may come in handy later. Pair up with a classmate and follow these four steps:

1. One of you reads the first vocabulary word aloud. Together, make sure that you understand the meaning of the word.

2. On a sheet of paper, write the word. Then write an example of when or how you might use this word in the future.

3. Repeat steps 1 and 2 for each word in the list.

4. In a class discussion, share some of your results. Point out any words that you don't see yourself using in the future—and prepare to be surprised and informed by how others *do* plan to use the words!

Master It: Use Words in Meaningful Ways

Did You Know?

Directions: In this activity, you will choose one vocabulary word to explore. Then you'll share a few facts about this word with your classmates. Follow these steps:

1. Review the list of vocabulary words and their meanings. Choose one word that seems most interesting to you.

2. Find **two or three** facts about the word that you can share with your class. For instance, what animals might be seen on a *safari*? What are synonyms of *vague*? Useful sources of information include textbooks, encyclopedias, friends, family members, and magazine articles.

3. Write a few sentences stating two or three facts about the vocabulary word. Here are some phrases that you could use to begin the sentences:

   > Did you know that . . .

   > A surprising fact about (*vocabulary word*) is . . .

   > A question I had about (*vocabulary word*) was . . .

4. Practice reading your sentences aloud. Then read your sentences to your classmates.

Vocabulary Mini-Lesson: Words Come from Mythology

Besides foreign languages, another interesting source of English words is Greek and Roman mythology. Mythology is the collection of myths, or stories that were created to explain how or why things exist. These stories usually involve gods and heroes. For example, in mythology there is a goddess of rainbows, Iris, and a god Apollo who drives the sun across the sky every day.

Many familiar words have their origin in people or creatures described in ancient myths. For example, the word *volcano* comes from Vulcan, the Roman god of fire. Can you guess why?

Words to Know: Vocabulary Lists and Activities

In this section, you'll learn ten words that come from Greek and Roman myths. You'll learn the myths these words came from as well as the more modern uses of the words.

List 15   Words from Mythology

Read each word, its origin, what it means, and how it's used.

Word	Its Origin	What It Means	How It's Used
herculean *(adj)* hur-kyuh-LEE-uhn	*Hercules* was a Greek hero who had superhuman strength.	very difficult or challenging	Constructing the Golden Gate Bridge was a *herculean* task.
hygiene *(n)* HIGH-jeen	*Hygeia* (high-JEE-uh) was the Greek goddess of health.	practices that help to ensure good health, such as cleanliness	Washing your hands before handling food is an important part of personal *hygiene*.
hypnosis *(n)* hip-NOH-sis	From *Hypnos*, the Greek god of sleep	a trancelike state in which (some people believe) a person is more easily influenced by others	Some people undergo *hypnosis* in order to quit smoking. A hypnotist puts the person into a trance and then convinces that person to quit.
martial *(adj)* MAHR-shuhl	From *Mars*, the Roman god of war	of, relating to, or suggestive of war or a warrior; warlike	My brother has been studying karate, tae kwon do, and other *martial* arts for five years.
Midas touch *(n)* MY-duhs tuhch	From the legend of King Midas, who was given the power to turn everything he touched into gold	someone who has an ability to make money very easily in any area he or she enters into	Joe never had formal business training, yet he has the *Midas touch*—every company he owns has become successful.
mnemonic *(adj)* ni-MON-ik	In Greek mythology, *Mnemosyne* (nih-MAH-sih-nee) was the goddess of memory.	assisting or helping memory	Our science teacher taught us a *mnemonic* device to help us remember the names of the planets: My Very Energetic Mother Just Served Us Nachos (Mercury, Venus, Earth, Mars, Jupiter, Saturn, Uranus, Neptune).
ogre *(n)* OH-ger	*Orcus* was the Roman god of the underworld (the underground home of the dead).	in fairy tales and folklore, a giant or monster	In the story, the horrible *ogre* threatened to eat the children.
panic *(n)* PAN-ik	*Pan* was a Greek god of fields and shepherds, who frightened people.	sudden, intense fear	Someone yelling "Fire!" caused *panic* in the movie theater.
psyche *(n)* SIGH-kee	Psyche was the wife of Cupid.	mind or soul	A therapist can help a person figure out what's going on in his or her *psyche*, beyond what he or she is aware of.
python *(n)* PIE-thon	In Greek mythology, *Python* was the name of a huge serpent.	a large snake found in Africa, Asia, and Australia	*Pythons* kill their prey by squeezing them.

Own It: Develop Your Word Understanding

Yes, It Is—No, It's Not

Directions: Work with a partner to complete the activity. For each organizer, complete these steps:

1. *What It Is:* In this box, state what the key word means in your own words.

2. *What It's Not:* In this box, list antonyms, expressions with an opposite meaning to the key word, or things/ideas that some-one may confuse with the key word. For example, *herculean* is not *easy*; a *python* is not a *cobra*; *psyche* is not *psychic*.

3. *Examples:* In this box, list examples of the key word. For instance, name ways to maintain good *hygiene* or recall a time that you *panicked*.

4. *Memory Cue:* Sketch a simple illustration to help you remem-ber the word's meaning.

what it is	what it's not

herculean

examples	memory cue

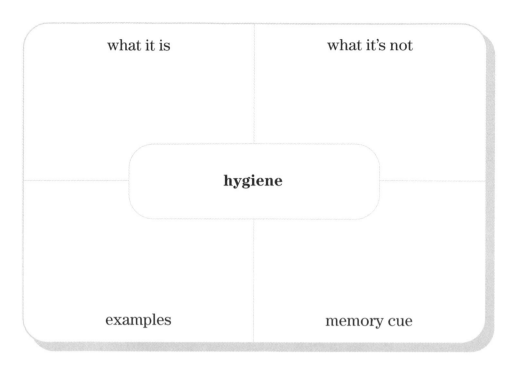

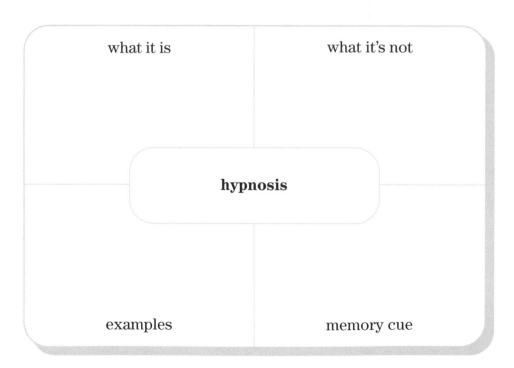

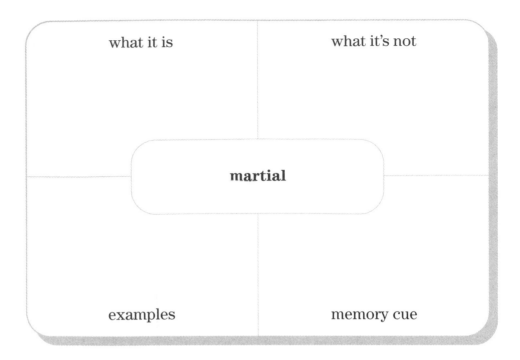

what it is

what it's not

martial

examples

memory cue

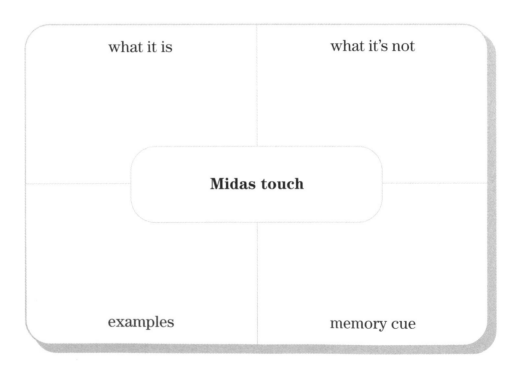

what it is

what it's not

Midas touch

examples

memory cue

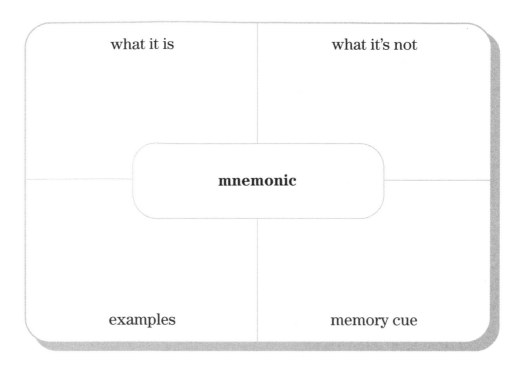

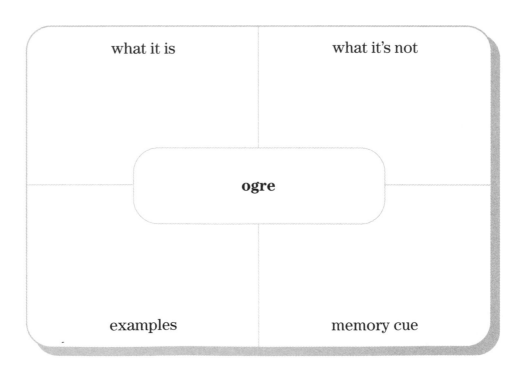

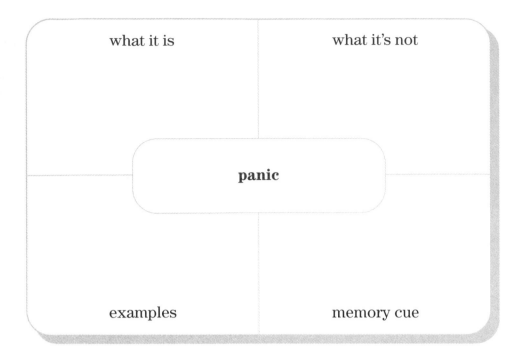

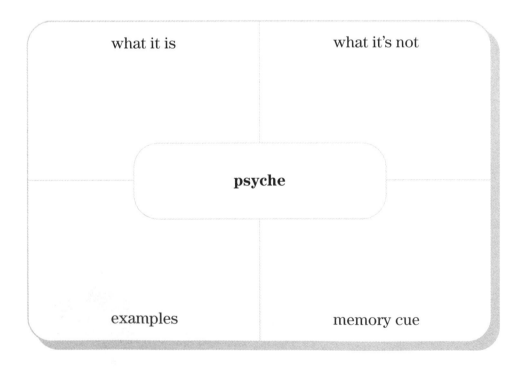

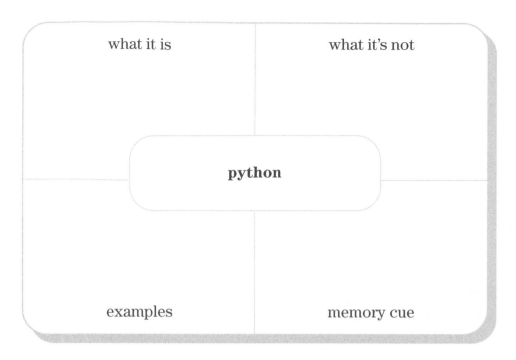

what it is	what it's not
	python	
examples	memory cue

I thought that studying for the science midterm would be a <u>herculean</u> task, but <u>mnemonic</u> devices helped prevent me from <u>panicking</u>...

Link It: Make Word-to-World Connections

Visiting Celebrity

Directions: Imagine that Hercules, Hygeia, Hypnos, Mars, King Midas, Mnemosyne, Orcus, Pan, Psyche, or Python is coming to visit your school. What do you think this "celebrity" would say to the students? What might be the purpose for the visit?

Create a poster announcing the upcoming visit of one of these characters. Your poster should inform students of the character's visit, the purpose of the event, and why students will want to attend. As a challenge, on your poster use the vocabulary word that is derived from the character's name.

When your poster is finished, display it in a classroom poster exhibit.

Master It: Use Words in Meaningful Ways

Take Two

Directions: Work in groups of five to complete the activity. Here's what to do:

1. Each of you takes two vocabulary words. Write down the two characters from mythology that are the origins of your words.

2. In a book of myths or another source, read the stories about your two characters. Think about why the modern word derived from the character's name.

3. Next, write a short summary of each myth. After each summary, explain the connection between the character's name and the modern word we get from the name.

4. Finally, share your summaries with your five-person group. In addition, your teacher may ask for volunteers to read a summary to the class.

Vocabulary Mini-Lesson: Words Are Named After People and Places

Did you know that the words *frankfurter* and *hamburger* both come from the names of German cities? *Frankfurter* gets its name from Frankfurt while *hamburger* is named after Hamburg.

Many other common words get their names from people and places. For example, the *Ferris wheel* is named after George Ferris, the engineer who designed the first one. Some of the words in this section may surprise you.

Words to Know: Vocabulary Lists and Activities

In this section, you'll learn ten words that come from famous people and places. You'll learn each word's origin and its more modern meaning.

List 16   Words from the Names of People and Places

Read each word, what it means, its origin, and how it's used.

Word	What It Means	Its Origin	How It's Used
academy *(n)* uh-KAD-uh-mee	a school, especially a private high school	from Greek *Akadēmeia*, the place where the ancient Greek philosopher Plato taught school	After graduating from the *academy*, Elizabeth went to college.
calico *(n)* KAL-i-ko	a cotton fabric	named after Calicut, India, from where the cloth was first made	Emma's dress was a colorful *calico* print.
derrick *(n)* DER-ik	a large crane used to lift and move heavy objects	named after Thomas Derrick, a 17th-century English hangman	Construction workers used a *derrick* to move the steel beam.
diesel *(n)* DEE-zuhl	a type of engine that burns fuel oil	named for Rudolph Diesel, a German inventor of the early 20th-century	The engine in this vehicle is a *diesel*, which uses less fuel than a gasoline engine.
duffel *(n)* DUH-full	a rough, heavy woolen material	Named for the town Duffel in Belgium	I packed some towels and sunscreen into my *duffel* bag and headed to the beach.
gauze *(n)* gawz	a thin, lightweight cloth	may be named for Gaza, Palestine, a city associated with its production; or, may come from the Arabic word for "silk"	The nurse wrapped the wound with a cotton *gauze*.
saxophone *(n)* SAK-suh-fohn	a woodwind instrument	named after Antoine Sax, 19th-century Belgium instrument maker who invented it	Max plays *saxophone* in the school band.
sideburns *(n)* SIDE-burnz	hair on the sides of the face	originally called "burnsides"; named for Ambrose Burnside, 19th-century Civil War general, known for his bushy whiskers	Some men like to grow long *sideburns*, while others trim them short.
tangerine *(n)* tan-juh-REEN	a sweet, juicy citrus fruit	named after Tangier, Morocco, from where it was first obtained	The *tangerine* looks like a small orange, but it is easier to peel.
watt *(n)* wot	a unit of electric or mechanical power	named for James Watt, a 19th-century Scottish engineer and inventor	This lamp uses a 60-*watt* bulb.

Did You Know?

As you learned from this chapter's Sneak Peek activity, a word that comes from or is based on the name of a real or imaginary person is called an eponym. For example, *sandwich* is an eponym that comes from the Earl of Sandwich, the 18th-century English nobleman who invented it.

Own It: Develop Your Word Understanding

Look It Up!

Directions: Work with a partner to complete the activity. Here's what to do:

1. Look up each vocabulary word in an encyclopedia, dictionary, or other reference source. Your goal? Find out something about each word that is not printed in the table in this book. For instance, by looking up *derrick*, you may learn what an oil derrick is. By looking up *sideburns*, you may find a picture of what sideburns look like.

2. Fill in the table by writing and/or drawing a piece of new information about each word.

3. In a class discussion, share some of the facts you learned.

Word	Something New I Learned About This Word
academy	
calico	
derrick	
diesel	
duffel	

continued

gauze	
saxophone	
sideburns	
tangerine	
watt	

Link It: Make Word-to-World Connections

It's All in Your Head

Directions: Work with a partner to complete these steps:

1. Your partner will read each vocabulary word aloud (from page 99). After you hear each word, write it in one of the columns in the table below.

2. Repeat step 2. Now *you* read the words to your partner.

This word is completely new to me.	I have heard this word, but I've never used it.	I have used this word before.

3. Compare lists. Talk about when you have heard these words before and how you have used them. Read the words in the first column aloud to help them become more familiar.

> Once, I tried to grow <u>sideburns</u>, but my new look was not very popular with my female classmates!

Master It: Use Words in Meaningful Ways

Let Me Introduce You

Directions: Each word in the vocabulary list derives from the name of a person or place. Choose one of these people or places to learn more about, and follow these steps:

1. Investigate the person or place you chose. For instance, look it up in an encyclopedia, find a book about it, or interview a knowledgeable person.

2. Write a one-page report called "Let Me Introduce You to (the person or place)." Your audience for this report is your classmates. Tell them some basic information about your topic so that they too will become familiar with it. If you find a photograph or drawing of the person or place, include a copy of it—or your own sketch based on the image.

3. Your teacher will collect everyone's reports and images and sort them into folders—one folder per person or place. Whenever you have a few free minutes in class, read some of the reports that your classmates composed.

Wrapping Up: Review What You've Learned

Here's a brief summary of what you've studied in this chapter.

> Many familiar words come from foreign languages. They have been added to English over the centuries and are still being added today. These words may not seem foreign, either because their form has changed or because we are so used to hearing them.

> Many words have their origin in people or creatures described in Greek and Roman mythology.

> Some common words are based on the names of people and places.

Chapter Review Exercises

Flaunt It: Show Your Word Understanding

In the following exercises, you'll demonstrate your understanding of each vocabulary word. You will use vocabulary words, or forms of the words, to complete sentences and to write sentences of your own.

A Sentence Completion

Directions: Circle the letter of the word that best completes each sentence.

1. After drying in the sun, the _____ blocks were used to construct a sturdy wall around the yard.

   a. adobe **b.** bronze
   c. calico **d.** herculean

2. Would you like one of these _____ on the upcoming folk-life festival?

   a. souvenirs **b.** bouquets
   c. charities **d.** brochures

3. In my study of prehistoric animals, I became fascinated by a huge, tusked creature called a/an _____.

   a. ogre **b.** sideburn
   c. mammoth **d.** derrick

4. After developing an interest in woodwind instruments, Camille signed up for _____ lessons.

   a. ballet **b.** hygiene
   c. saxophone **d.** vague

5. In the navy, my uncle has risen to the position of _____ after years of dedicated service.

   a. watt **b.** admiral
   c. academy **d.** attorney

B Word Choice

Directions: Underline the word that best completes each sentence.

6. When I was on the (*sofa, safari*) in Africa, I saw giraffes, elephants, and crocodiles.

7. A monstrous (*tornado, typhoon*) swept across Kansas, flattening trees and fences.

8. One hot day I saw something shimmering up ahead on the asphalt; it was a (*mirage, yacht*) that disappeared when I got closer.

9. This Friday, my friends and I plan to watch a scary movie about jungle explorers who are pursued by a slithering (*python, mammoth*).

10. Let me put some (*diesel, gauze*) on that wound for you.

 ## Writing

Directions: Write one or more sentences to answer each of the following questions. Be sure to use the italicized vocabulary word in your sentence. Write your sentences on a separate sheet of paper.

11. What is your *attitude* toward team sports?

12. Have you ever slid down a *banister*?

13. Have you ever worn a *shawl*?

14. What is one thing that could make you *panic*?

15. Would you rather go on a *yacht* or a *safari*?

Chapter Extension Activities

Activities à la Carte: Extend Your Word Knowledge

The activities on this page are presented à la carte, like items on a restaurant menu, meaning that you can choose from a variety of options. Your teacher may assign an activity or let you pick the one that tempts your appetite. If time allows, you might do more than one activity. All of the activities feature the same ingredient: **words derived from foreign words, mythology, people, or places**. Dig in!

Because I Say So

Pair up with a friend and stage a five-minute debate based on a vocabulary word. For instance, should people be allowed to kill animals on a *safari*? Should people give money to *charity*? To see whose argument was stronger, ask for a show of hands in the audience.

Yellow Pages

For a week, study your world for examples of modern uses of names from mythology. Look at brand names, company names (try the yellow pages in a phone book), signs, and billboards. Ask people for examples that they know of. Report back to the class and offer your answer to this question: Why do names from ancient myths remain so alive today?

 ### Come Again?

Translate a selection of words in Lists 13 and 14 (pages 85 and 88) back into their languages of origin. Make a table of the results to display in the classroom. For an added challenge, include some words derived from foreign languages that are not listed in this chapter.

Because This Is My Cause

Choose a cause near and dear to you, and write a *brochure* to promote it. For topic ideas, peruse the vocabulary words—*charity*, for instance, or *ballet*, *tornado*, or *saxophone*. For creative inspiration, look at brochures found in libraries, offices, or other places. Notice that brochures usually are laid out on folded paper and have a combination of words and images.

Telling Stories

Choose a Greek or Roman myth that younger kids would enjoy. Arrange with a teacher or librarian to present this myth to a group of kids. Practice telling or reading the myth aloud (you could research tips for reading aloud). If possible, prepare at least one visual such as a poster or illustrations to grab your listeners' interest. If you enjoy the spotlight, perhaps you are destined for a career as an entertainer, teacher, or public speaker.

My Eponym

If you could coin a new word based on your name, what would it be? What would this new word mean, and why would it derive from your name? Play around with your own name and the names of your friends. Create a list of eponyms, complete with definitions. If you're enjoying yourself, create an entire class directory of eponyms.

One of a Kind—or One of Many?

How special are the words listed in this chapter? When people need to use the exact right word, do these words stand out as one of a kind? Or are they one of many equally useful choices? Develop your opinion on this issue by grabbing a thesaurus and looking up vocabulary words. Does each vocabulary word have synonyms? Are the synonyms equally precise, expressive, or unique? Overall, do you think English is richer because of words derived from other languages and people's names, or simply more cluttered?

Learning New and Special Words

6

The world is a BIG place. In fact, you can think of the world as a container for lots of smaller worlds. For instance, there's your world—the people and places you see every day, the things you do, the way you talk. Then there are other worlds—say, the world of science, technology, medicine, or law.

Just as you and your friends use words and expressions that may not make sense to outsiders, specialized communities use specialized words or terms. When you first hear these terms, they may seem unfamiliar or even unpronounceable. But by becoming familiar with these words, you open doors to other worlds—worlds you may love to visit, to study, or to make your own.

In this chapter, you'll learn vocabulary words from some of these worlds. As you study them, think about how your world and these other worlds can meet. It could be a life-changing experience!

Objectives

In this chapter, you will learn

> How and why our language expands

> New words from technology, science, and pop culture

> Words from the specific areas of medicine and law

Sneak Peek: Preview the Lesson

The Best of All Worlds

Think about your world and your language. When you're with friends and family, what words and expressions do you use that "the outside world" may not use? Write some of these words in the circle on the next page labeled "My World."

Next, read the words in the outer circles. These are some of the words that you'll study in this chapter. If any of these words fit into your world, write them in the center circle as well. Chances are, your personal world already shares elements with at least one other world!

science/technology

high-def
icon
Internet
wireless

new words

fantabulous
hazmat
spam
surf

my world

medicine

allergy
asthma
farsighted
sprain

the law

jury
plea
trespass
witness

Vocabulary Mini-Lesson: How Our Language Expands

The English language is always growing and changing. New words are added, and old words take on new or changed meanings. Consider a word like *mouse*, for example. Fifty years ago, when people used the word, they were referring to the fuzzy little creature that cats chase. Today, when you hear the word *mouse*, you probably think of the device used to move the cursor on a computer screen.

Some new words are formed by blending other words. The word *brunch* combines letters from <u>br</u>eakfast and <u>lunch</u>. *Smog* combines letters from <u>sm</u>oke and <u>fog</u>. Other words enter our language through technology and science, or through the fields of medicine and law. Think about the words *e-mail*, *cell phone*, *laptop*, and *laser*. These words did not exist until the items were created. Dictionaries are constantly being revised and updated as our language changes and grows.

Words to Know: Vocabulary Lists and Activities

The first two lists in this section contain relatively new words that came into being for various reasons, such as changes in technology and science, and trends in pop culture. The last two lists contain words from medicine and law that cross over into general use.

List 17   Technology and Science Words

Here are ten new words from technology and science. Read each word, what it means, and how it's used.

Word	What It Means	How It's Used
global warming *(n)* GLOWH-bul WORE-ming	a gradual increase in Earth's temperature, generally believed to be caused by pollution	Scientists fear that *global warming* will melt the polar ice caps and cause widespread flooding.
google *(v)* GOO-gul	to use the Google search engine to find information about someone or something online (see *search engine* below)	Jenny *googled* the author to learn more about his life and the books he had written.
high-def *(adj)* high-DEF	(short for *high-definition*) a system that offers high-quality images with greater detail than standard images	Our new *high-def* television set has a wonderfully sharp picture.
icon *(n)* EYE-kon	a symbol or picture	The *icons* displayed on the screen correspond to different functions that the computer can perform.
Internet *(n)* IN-ter-net	the worldwide network of computers; often referred to simply as *the Net* (To review the prefix *inter-,* see page 4.)	Millions of computers communicate with each other over the *Internet*.
online *(adv, adj)* ON-LAHYN	through a computer network	Tania likes to use her computer to shop *online* for books and other items.
search engine *(n)* surch EN-juhn	computer software used to search for information on the Web	A *search engine* enables you to find information about specific topics.

continued

space shuttle *(n)* speys SHUHT-l	a spacecraft designed for shuttling people and equipment between Earth and a space station	The *space shuttle* transported the astronauts to the International Space Station.
Web *(n)* web	(short for *World Wide Web*) a system of interconnected Internet sites, offering text, graphics, and sound	The company's *Web* site provides information about its products.
wireless *(adj)* WIRE-lis	operating without needing to be connected with wires (To review the suffix *-less,* see page 37.)	The cell phone is a form of *wireless* communication.

Did You Know?

Some words that are trademarked brand names referring to a specific product are commonly used to refer to *any* similar product. Examples include *Kleenex, Xerox,* and *Jell-O.*

The word *google* is a little different. *Google* is a trademark that started as a noun and has now become a commonly used verb. However, its meaning is still limited specifically to the Google search engine, rather than to *any* search engine.

Own It: Develop Your Word Understanding

Accept or Reject?

Directions: In this activity, you'll spot fake definitions of the vocabulary words. Here's how the activity works:

1. Your teacher will assign you one of the vocabulary words. On an index card, write your name and the word you received. On the back of the card, write two things: a *correct* definition of the word and an *incorrect* definition that you make up. (Label each definition.)

2. Your teacher will mix everyone's cards together in a box.

3. Your teacher will pull out a card and read the vocabulary word aloud. Then he or she will read *one* of the definitions on the card. You must decide if the definition is correct or incorrect.

4. Your teacher will ask for a show of hands to indicate whether you *accept* or *reject* the definition. Be prepared to defend your vote!

Link It: Make Word-to-World Connections

Thinking of You

Directions: When it comes to technology and science words, especially new terms, some people are clueless. Do you know someone like this? In this activity, you'll write a letter to a "clueless" person explaining several vocabulary words. Here's what to do:

1. Review the list of vocabulary words. As you do so, think about someone you know who may be unfamiliar with some of these words. Choose **three** words to work with.

2. Write a letter to the person you chose. In the letter, mention that you are studying technology and science words. Suggest that this person may like to know about a few of these words. Then explain the meaning of each word and give an example of how the person might use it in his or her own life.

3. Share a copy of the letter with your teacher. Whether or not you send the letter to its addressee is up to you!

Master It: Use Words in Meaningful Ways

Have a Conversation

Directions: In this activity, you and your classmates will have a conversation with your teacher. The goal is to use as many vocabulary words as possible during the conversation. Here's how it works:

1. Your teacher will divide the class into teams.

2. Your teacher will get a conversation started by reading one of these prompts:

> I wonder if any of these terms will become outdated in the next 20 years.

> I wonder which of these things will have the biggest impact on the lives of people in this room.

3. Raise your hand to signal that you want to share in the conversation. Then state a sentence that uses a vocabulary word *and* that makes sense in the conversation.

4. When one or more conversations are finished, your teacher will add up each team's points and declare a winner.

List 18   New Words and Meanings

Here are ten additional new words from a variety of sources, including culture, sports, law, and entertainment. Read each word, what it means, and how it's used.

Word	What It Means	How It's Used
barista *(n)* bahr-EE-stuh	a person who makes and serves coffee drinks for customers	My sister got a job as a *barista* at a café to make extra money during the holidays.
cybercrime *(n)* SIGH-ber-krime	criminal activities carried out through the use of computers or the Internet	Theft of personal information is one kind of *cybercrime*.
edutainment *(n)* ej-oo-TAYN-muhnt	entertainment (TV shows, movies, games) that are meant to be educational	This computer game is a form of *edutainment*; it teaches kids how to do addition while they're pretending to work in a candy store.
fantabulous *(adj)* fan-TAB-yuh-luhs	(blend of *fantastic* and *fabulous*) outstandingly good; excellent	The food in this Italian restaurant is *fantabulous*!
ginormous *(adj)* jih-NOR-muhs	(blend of *gigantic* and *enormous*) extremely large	With the money he earned, Mr. Johnson bought a *ginormous* new house.
hazmat *(adj)* HAS-matt	(short for *hazardous material*) dangerous substances	Police called in a *hazmat* team to investigate the contents of the shipping container.
sitcom *(n)* SIT-kom	(short for *situation comedy*) a comedy series that involves the same cast of characters in a succession of episodes	The star of the *sitcom* went on to have a successful movie career.
spam *(n)* spam	worthless e-mail, usually advertisements, sent to large numbers of people	Many computer users complain that they receive too much *spam* in their mailboxes.

continued

supercross *(n)* SOO-per-kross	a motorcycle race that includes high jumps and is usually held on a dirt track indoors	I got chills when I saw the competitor fall off his bike during the *supercross*; luckily, he was okay.
surf *(v)* surf	to browse or scan, looking for something of interest	My brother likes to channel *surf*, using the remote to find sports shows on TV, but I'd rather *surf* the Web.

Own It: Develop Your Word Understanding

Your Fantabulous Life

Directions: Write your answer to each question on the lines provided.

1. Name something about yourself that is *fantabulous*.

   _____

2. If a *sitcom* were based on your life, what main characters would it include?

   _____

3. Would you rather have a *ginormous* bank account or *ginormous* generosity?

   _____

4. Which room in your house most needs a *hazmat* warning on the door (if only as a joke)?

   _____

5. What can you do to avoid *cybercrime*?

   _____

6. What do you do with *spam*?

   _____

7. How would you prefer to *surf*—on a board, with a remote, or with a keyboard?

   _____

8. Of all the TV shows you watched as a child, which ones would be considered *edutainment*?

   _____

9. Would you ever participate in a risky sport like *supercross*?

   _____

10. Would you rather work as a *barista* or in a clothing store?

   _____

The <u>barista</u> at the coffee shop around the corner knows me. Once a week, I go there after school and order a <u>ginormous</u> brownie—they're <u>fantabulous</u>. Sometimes I bring my laptop and do homework, since there's a wireless connection. It's all good!

Link It: Make Word-to-World Connections

Connotations

Directions: Every word has a *denotation*, which means its dictionary definition. In addition, many words have a *connotation*, which is the meaning *suggested* by personal responses to the word. For example, *steak* is a piece of meat. That's the denotation. To some people, steak has a positive (pleasant) connotation—yum! To others, steak has a negative (unpleasant) connotation—Eww! I can't believe someone would eat that!

Look at the vocabulary words in the list. Which ones have positive connotations for you? Which ones have negative connotations? In the organizers on the following pages, classify each word's connotation. Then explain your answer. The first one has been done for you. *Note: You'll learn more about denotation and connotation in Chapter 9.*

barista	explanation of connotation
connotation hip, cool	The word "barista" sounds fancy to me and makes me think of a cool college kid working at a gourmet cafe, not a regular deli.

cybercrime

connotation

explanation of connotation

edutainment

connotation

explanation of connotation

fantabulous

connotation

explanation of connotation

ginormous

connotation

explanation of connotation

hazmat

connotation

explanation of connotation

| sitcom | explanation of connotation |
| connotation | |

| spam | explanation of connotation |
| connotation | |

| supercross | explanation of connotation |
| connotation | |

| surf | explanation of connotation |
| connotation | |

Master It: Use Words in Meaningful Ways

This Is Like That

Directions: Each analogy on the next page expresses a relationship, such as opposites or purpose. (The *Hint* tells you the relationship.) Notice that an analogy has two halves, separated by a double colon (::). You may want to circle this double colon to make the separation more obvious.

Your job is to complete each analogy. To do so, think about the first two words and how they relate. Then look at the second part of the analogy. You are given one word and must fill in another word. Ask yourself, What word relates to the given word in the same way that the first two words relate?

Example: sitcom : funny :: drama : <u>serious   </u>
    Hint: A sitcom may be described as funny.

1. cybercrime : identity theft :: traffic crime : _____
    Hint: Identity theft is a type of cybercrime.

2. fantabulous : awful :: sharp : _____
    Hint: Fantabulous and awful are antonyms.

3. ginormous : huge :: fearful : _____
    Hint: Ginormous and huge are synonyms.

4. hazmat team : protect :: football team : _____
    Hint: The purpose of a hazmat team is to protect.

5. sitcom : television :: play : _____
    Hint: A sitcom is seen on television.

6. spam : sell :: joke : _____
    Hint: The purpose of spam is to sell something.

7. surf : surfing :: think : _____
    Hint: The present tense of surf is surfing.

List 19   Medical Words

The following words are commonly used to describe medical problems or conditions. Read each word, what it means, and how it's used.

Word	What It Means	How It's Used
allergy *(n)* AL-er-jee	unusual reaction to a particular substance, such as a food, pollen, or dust (The substance causing the reaction is an *allergen*.)	Brody must watch what he eats because he has a severe *allergy* to peanuts.
asthma *(n)* AZ-muh	disease characterized by breathing difficulty, wheezing, and coughing	Most people can control their *asthma* by taking medicine.

continued

farsighted *(adj)* FAHR-sigh-tid	better able to see distant objects than objects nearby	People who are *farsighted* may need to wear glasses for reading.
fever *(n)* FEE-ver	a body temperature that is higher than normal	A sick child may run a high *fever*.
internal *(adj)* in-TUR-nl	of or arising within a person or being (In medicine, *internal* can specifically mean given or applied by being swallowed.)	I thought the redness on my arms was the result of having worn an itchy sweater, but my doctor said that it had an *internal* cause—it was an allergic reaction to something I ate.
nearsighted *(adj)* NEER-sigh-tid	better able to see objects that are nearby than objects at a distance	*Nearsighted* students may need glasses to see the board clearly.
prescription *(n)* pri-SKRIP-shuhn	a doctor's written directions for the amount and use of a medicine (To review the root *script*, see page 56.)	We brought the *prescription* for cough medicine to the drugstore.
sprain *(n)* spreyn	an injury to a ligament (tissue that connects bones) by twisting or wrenching	Caitlyn was worried that she had broken her ankle doing gymnastics, but it was only a *sprain*.
symptom *(n)* SIMP-tuhm	a condition that indicates or results from a disease or other disorder	A sore throat and runny nose may be *symptoms* of a cold.
ward *(n)* wawrd	a division in a hospital, usually where patients with a similar condition are treated	The children's cancer *ward* at the hospital was very welcoming to visitors.

Own It: Develop Your Word Understanding

Exploring Key Words

Directions: Work with a partner to complete the activity. Each of you completes five of the ten graphic organizers on the next pages. Then share your results. For each graphic organizer, follow three steps.

1. Study each vocabulary word at the top and review its definition on pages 119–120. Then use your own words and ideas to write a definition in the center box.

2. Use your knowledge of suffixes and plurals to create other forms of the word. (For instance, add *-less* to *symptom* to form *symptomless*.) Write these words in the first box.

3. In the third box, sketch or write a clue to help you remember the key word's meaning.

allergy

other word forms   my definition   memory cue

asthma

other word forms   my definition   memory cue

farsighted

other word forms   my definition   memory cue

fever

other word forms   my definition   memory cue

nearsighted

other word forms	my definition	memory cue

prescription

other word forms	my definition	memory cue

sprain

other word forms	my definition	memory cue

symptom

other word forms	my definition	memory cue

internal

other word forms	my definition	memory cue

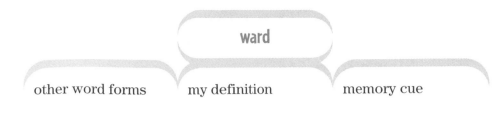

ward

| other word forms | my definition | memory cue |

Link It: Make Word-to-World Connections

The Doctor Is In

Directions: In this activity, you'll pretend to have *symptoms* of an injury or a condition named in the vocabulary list. Can you be convincing enough for a classmate to make the correct diagnosis? Follow these steps:

1. Form small groups. Choose an injury or condition from the word list and think about its *symptoms*.

2. Imagine that your group members are your personal medical staff. Explain your symptoms in detail, using words or body language—but do not name your condition. How long does it take for someone to diagnose your problem correctly?

3. Once your condition is diagnosed, listen to other people's symptoms. For added fun, write *prescriptions* for group members.

I told my mom I had <u>symptoms</u> of a cold, like the chills and a <u>fever</u>, but she knew I was faking it. She told me I didn't need a <u>prescription</u> for medicine; I just needed to go to school!

Master It: Use Words in Meaningful Ways

Memo from Me

Directions: Imagine that you are the school nurse and you have just seen three different members of a school athletic team. Their condition may be found in the vocabulary list on pages 119–120. Now you must write a memo to the athletes' coach. Your purpose is to inform the coach of the players' conditions and to state whether each athlete can attend practice this week.

Use the blank memo form below to write your memo.

MEMO

TO: _____

FROM: _____

DATE: _____

SUBJECT: _____

_____

_____

_____

_____

_____

_____

_____

_____

_____

_____

_____

List 20 Legal Words

The following ten words are commonly used to describe legal situations—situations involving the law. Read each word, what it means, and how it's used.

Word	What It Means	How It's Used
allege (v) uh-LEJ	to state or claim something before proving or without proving	She *alleged* that this man stole her wallet, but she didn't have any proof that it was him.
attorney general (n) uh-TUR-nee JEN-er-uhl	the chief law officer of a nation or state (plural: *attorneys general*) (To review the word *attorney,* see List 13, page 85.)	The U.S. *attorney general* serves as legal adviser to the president.
felony (n) FEL-uh-nee	a serious crime for which the punishment may be a prison sentence of more than one year, or even death	The burglary was considered a *felony* and the sentence was four years in prison.
jury (n) JOOR-ee	a group of citizens chosen to serve in a court of law and give a decision based on the evidence presented	The members of the *jury* were convinced that the woman had committed the crime.
plea (n) plee	something that is alleged or begged in defense, or as an excuse; a genuine request for help or sympathy	He made a *plea* to his parents to go easy on him and not ground him for breaking the rules.
trespass (v) TRES-pass	to enter another person's land or property without the person's permission	The sign warned people not to *trespass* on the field because it was private property.
trial (n) TRY-uhl	a formal examination of a case in a court of law to determine whether the charge or claim made is true	Lawyers for both sides asked many questions during the long *trial*.
uphold (v) uhp-HOHLD	to support or keep up	I always *uphold* the dog cleanup law, and I clean up after my Lab Max.
verdict (n) VUR-dikt	the decision of a judge or jury	The jury reached a *verdict* of not guilty in the trial of the man accused of robbery.
witness (n) WIT-nis	a person who makes sworn statements in court as to what he or she has seen or heard	The *witness* said that she saw the accused thief enter the building.

Own It: Develop Your Word Understanding

Mix and Match

Directions: In this activity, you will mingle with classmates, trying to match vocabulary words with their definitions. Here's what to do:

1. Your teacher will write each vocabulary word on an index card. On separate cards, he or she will write the definitions. Then the cards will be jumbled together in a box.

2. You will pull one card from the box. You'll have either a vocabulary word or a definition.

3. Move around the classroom to find the person who has the definition of your vocabulary word, or the word that goes with your definition.

4. In a class discussion, explain how easy or difficult it was to make the match. Which words or definitions made you think hard about whether they were a correct match? Which were easier to eliminate?

Link It: Make Word-to-World Connections

Ask an Expert

Directions: In this activity, you'll become an "expert" on two vocabulary words. Then you'll exchange information with experts on different words. Follow these steps:

1. Your teacher will assign you one of these sets of questions:

> 1. a. Who is the *attorney general* of the United States?
>   b. What is the difference between a *felony* and a *misdemeanor*?
> 2. a. How many people serve on a *jury*?
>   b. In a jury, which person states the *verdict* to the judge?
> 3. a. What is a school rule that your administrators would *uphold*?
>   b. What kind of *trespass* rules does your school have?
> 4. a. In what building are *trials* held in your town or city?
>   b. During a trial, who asks the *witnesses* questions?

2. Find the answer to your questions. Helpful resources include library books, a Web site recommended by a teacher or librarian, and knowledgeable people.

3. Meet with the other experts on your two vocabulary words and verify that everyone has found correct information.

4. Form new groups of four people—one expert for each set of questions.

5. As the expert on your questions, share the information you found.

Master It: Use Words in Meaningful Ways

Long Arm of the Law

Directions: If you formed a student court of law at your school, how would it work? What kinds of "crimes" would bring students to your court? Who would be the judge? The jury? The witnesses? What kinds of punishment would follow the verdict?

1. In a small group, brainstorm ideas based on these and other questions.

2. Together, prepare a description of the ideal student court of law. (To divide up the work, you can break the description into sections.) Be sure to use vocabulary words! (Refer to page 125.)

3. Present your work to the class. You can use one spokesperson from your group or take turns speaking.

4. Reflect on what you heard. How is your ideal court similar to those of other groups? How is it different? After hearing other ideas, would you change anything in your own court of law?

Wrapping Up: Review What You've Learned

Here's a brief summary of what you've studied in this chapter.

> Our language is constantly growing and changing. New words are added, while old words take on new or changed meanings.

> Some new words are formed by blending other words. Other words enter our language through technology and science.

> There are many medical and legal words that people use in everyday conversation, hear on television and in the movies, and read in newspapers and magazines.

Chapter Review Exercises

Flaunt It: Show Your Word Understanding

In the following exercises, you'll demonstrate your understanding of each vocabulary word. You will use vocabulary words, or forms of the words, to complete sentences and to write sentences of your own.

A Sentence Completion

Directions: Circle the letter of the word that best completes each sentence.

1. Horace _____ his own name to find out if any Web sites mentioned him.

   a. surfed   **b.** googled
   c. witnessed   **d.** spammed

2. In the spring, my _____ to certain pollens causes me to sneeze a lot.

   a. symptom   **b.** asthma
   c. allergy   **d.** fever

3. For a lesson in our state's justice system, Mrs. Rochester took us on a field trip to the office of the _____.

   a. cybercrime   **b.** felony
   c. jury   **d.** attorney general

4. My parents like to rent _____ on DVD and watch them while eating popcorn and laughing.

   a. spam   **b.** Webs
   c. icons   **d.** sitcoms

5. Are any movies from the 1980s available in _____?

   a. spam   **b.** wireless
   c. high-def   **d.** google

B Word Choice

Directions: You are given two italicized words. Write each word, or a form of the word, on the appropriate blank to complete the sentence.

6. Because I am _____ , I must wear glasses for reading; however, my _____ mom wears glasses for driving. (*farsighted, nearsighted*)

7. Which _____ do you use to search the
   _____ for homework help? (*Web, search
   engine*)

8. Julia's _____ birthday cake tasted
   _____, and everyone enjoyed a second slice.
   (*ginormous, fantabulous*)

9. After a lengthy _____ , the jury worked together to reach a fair _____. (*verdict, trial*)

10. A/an _____ on the _____ suit
    helped identify its purpose of protecting against dangerous
    substances. (*icon, hazmat*)

C Writing

Directions: Follow the directions to write sentences using vocabulary words. Write your sentences on a separate sheet of paper.

11. Use *global warming* in a question that you could ask a science
    teacher.

12. Use *space shuttle* to make a statement about space travel.

13. Use *prescription* to tell about a visit to a doctor.

14. Use *sprain* in a description of an accident.

15. Use *trespass* in an imperative sentence (a sentence that makes
    a command).

Chapter Extension Activities

Activities à la Carte: Extend Your Word Knowledge

The activities on this page are presented à la carte, like items on a restaurant menu, meaning that you can choose from a variety of options. Your teacher may assign an activity or let you pick the one that tempts your appetite. If time allows, you might do more than one activity. All of the activities feature the same ingredient: **new and special words**. Dig in!

Show-and-Tell

Do you miss the good old days of show and tell, back when you were little? Well, it's time to revive that practice. Your assignment? With your teacher's/school's permission, bring in a *person* to show and tell about. This person must be connected in some way to one or more vocabulary words in this chapter. Perhaps you can introduce your class to a judge, a software programmer, or a baker who makes ginormous cookies. (Cookie samples are optional.)

Rock My World

If you are musically inclined, set some words from this chapter to music. You can rock them, rap them, croon them, chant them, or give them the blues. It's up to you!

Order in the Court!

Have you ever been inside a courtroom? What did it look like? Ask an adult to help you visit a courtroom or to find a video or pictures showing the insides of courtrooms. Then get your art supplies and create a diagram of a courtroom to show classmates. Label important elements, such as the jury box. Place people, such as lawyers and witnesses, where they would be during a trial.

You're Funarious

This lesson included several words that were formed by blending other words. Remember *fantabulous* and *ginormous*? Play around with words and make your own list of new words, complete with definitions. Entertain your friends with the results.

 ### Does That Translate?

Complete the activity above, except do the work in a language besides English. Use your knowledge of another language to blend new words and create definitions. Then share the results with someone who speaks the language. Chances are, your English-speaking classmates would enjoy hearing about the results too.

Brave New World

Did your study of new and specialized words spark an interest in a world outside your own? Find a way to explore this world. You could interview a professional, research articles and books, watch a video, or read news coverage. Based on your findings, prepare an oral report for your class. Your purpose is to persuade classmates that this world has a place for them in it.

A Mouse by Any Other Name

If you know a second language, search that language for new words and meanings. Can you identify new or blended words in that language that don't have English translations? What about the list of new words and meanings in this chapter—do any of them translate into the other language and keep the same meaning?

Mock Trial

Did you enjoy the Long Arm of the Law activity in this chapter (page 127)? Get some friends together and stage a mock trial. Use ideas from the activity to give structure to your trial. You can use the trial to draw attention to a rule at school that you think is necessary—or ridiculous.

Learning Words from Context

7

Imagine that someone asks you, "Do you like naan?" You might look at the person blankly, or say, "Huh?"

In contrast, imagine that someone asks you, "Do you like naan, or does Indian bread not appeal to you?" In this case, clues in the sentence help you know that naan is a type of bread.

Often, listening and reading are acts of "decoding." You face an unfamiliar word, and it's like a secret code. To crack the code, you examine the other words around the unfamiliar one. Then you make an educated guess about the word's meaning. This chapter will teach you different ways of cracking the codes of unfamiliar words. You may want to add some of the fascinating words you study to your permanent vocabulary.

Objectives

In this chapter, you will learn

> How context clues can help you determine the meanings of unknown words

> Six ways to use context clues

> Words from fiction, science, and history passages that you'll figure out yourself

Sneak Peek: Preview the Lesson

Appetizer

As you may know, an *appetizer* is a small sampling of food that whets your appetite for the meal to follow. Grab a partner and complete this lesson "appetizer" activity together.

First, one person skims the word lists in this chapter and reads some words aloud. Ten words is a good number to work with.

As your partner reads each word, record it in the appropriate column below. Return the favor by skimming the word lists and reading ten words aloud for your partner.

Finally, complete the sentence at the bottom of the table.

Note: The word lists are on pages 143, 147–8, 153–4 and 159–60.

I have used this word before.	I have heard this word but not used it.	This word is totally new to me.

In some of the passages in this chapter, I predict that I'll read about . . .

ocabulary Mini-Lesson: Using Context Clues

When you're reading, you may come upon a word whose meaning you're not sure about. A writer may use descriptive words that are new to you. Or an article in a magazine or online may contain unfamiliar terms. In situations like these, context clues can help you figure out the meaning of the unknown words.

Context is the group of words or sentences that comes before and after a particular word. Sometimes you need very little context, maybe just a phrase, to figure out a word. Other times, you may have to consider a whole paragraph to find the clues needed to understand a word's meaning.

Here's an example of how context clues work. Imagine you see the following announcement on the Web.

"Temperatures are falling rapidly. When they drop below freezing, wet roadways will have patches of ice. Drivers are warned to use extra care. The road conditions will be hazardous."

The word *hazardous* may be unfamiliar to you. However, the fact that drivers are being "warned" about "patches of ice" on the roads suggests that driving may be unsafe. From these context clues, you can figure out that *hazardous* means "dangerous."

Context clues take various forms. For example, a writer may make a word's meaning clear by giving examples. Or the writer may provide an explanation of a term, as in a science textbook. Sometimes a writer suggests the meaning of a word by making a comparison. You'll see examples of these kinds of context clues and others in the next section.

Did You Know?

The word *context* comes from a Latin word meaning "to weave together." It contains the prefix *con-*, which you learned in Chapter 1, page 4.

Six Ways to Use Context Clues

1. Examine the Descriptive Details

The details a writer includes when describing something offer important clues to word meaning. Notice the descriptive details in the following passage. Can you figure out the meaning of the underlined word from these details?

From Raul's <u>lofty</u> perch on the mountain, he could see for miles in every direction. The houses in the valley below looked tiny, and the people were barely visible. The bright blue sky seemed almost close enough to touch.

The descriptive details tell you the meaning of *lofty*. From Raul's place "on the mountain," he can "see for miles in every direction."

He is so high up that houses "looked tiny" and "people were barely visible." The sky seemed "almost close enough to touch." Based on these context clues, you can figure out that *lofty* means "very high."

Here's another example. What descriptive details help you figure out the meaning of the underlined word in this passage?

Sarah thought that babysitting the twins would be easy. She soon learned just how wrong she was. Both of the kids clamored for her attention as soon as their parents were out the door. They shouted and cried and pulled on her arms. They asked again and again for candy, ice cream, and anything else they could think of. After an hour, Sarah's head was ready to explode.

List three descriptive details that provide clues to the meaning of *clamored*.

a. _____

b. _____

c. _____

Based on the context clues you listed, what do you think *clamored* means? Write an explanation or a definition.

_____

2. Look for an Explanation or a Definition

Writers often explain or define a word when they use it. Look at these examples. What does the underlined word mean? How do you know?

When Stephanie broke her leg, she was taken to an orthopedist, a doctor who specializes in the treatment of bones, joints, and muscles.

Based on the definition in this sentence, what do you think an *orthopedist* is?

_____

_____

> The two men were <u>migrant</u> workers. They moved around from place to place, taking on whatever farmwork they could find.

Based on the explanation in the second sentence, you can tell that a *migrant* worker is a worker who _____

3. Search for Examples

Looking at the examples a writer gives can help you figure out the meaning of an unfamiliar word. The examples may appear in the same sentence as the word or in a separate sentence.

> ### Tip
>
> When writers give examples, they often use one of these phrases:
>
> for example   for instance   such as

Read this sentence, which uses examples as clues to the meaning of *vessels*.

> Handmade <u>vessels</u> such as jars, bowls, and cups fetched high prices at the art show.

What examples in the sentence help you figure out the meaning of *vessels*?

_____

Based on the examples in the sentence, what do you think a *vessel* is? Write an explanation or a definition.

_____

Now look at another passage that uses examples as context clues.

My dad is always quoting <u>proverbs</u>. One of his favorites is, "Never judge a book by its cover." He also likes, "Don't count your chickens before they're hatched."

What examples does the writer provide that help you figure out what a *proverb* is?

a. _____

b. _____

Based on the examples, what do you think a *proverb* is? Write an explanation or a definition.

_____

4. Look for Synonyms

A **synonym** is a word that means the same or almost the same as another word. For example, *big* is a synonym for *large*, and *happy* is a synonym for *glad*. Synonyms can be good context clues. Look at these examples. Can you find the synonyms for the underlined words?

The stone statue was <u>colossal</u>, so huge that we could hardly believe our eyes.

What is a synonym of *colossal*? _____
Now that you know what *colossal* means, use it in a sentence of your own.

_____

_____

John had a <u>morose</u> expression on his face. I wondered why he looked so miserable.

What is a synonym of *morose*? _____
Now that you know what *morose* means, use it in a sentence of your own.

_____

_____

5. Look for a Comparison

Writers may suggest a word's meaning by comparing one thing to another. Often, the comparisons use the word *like* or *as*.

To what is Carlos compared in the following sentence? How does this comparison help you understand the underlined word?

> Carlos, who is as brawny as a weight lifter, moved all the furniture into the truck in just an hour.

In the sentence, Carlos is compared to a _____.
How does the comparison help you understand the meaning of *brawny*?

_____

_____

What do you think *brawny* means?

_____

What comparison is made in the next sentence? (*Hint:* Look for the word *like*.) How does the comparison help you understand the underlined word?

> "I can't come to the party," Mandy said mournfully, sounding like a child who had lost her puppy.

In the sentence, Mandy is compared to a _____.
How does the comparison help you understand the meaning of *mournfully*?

_____

_____

What do you think *mournfully* means?

_____

6. Look for a Contrast

While a comparison shows how two things are similar, a **contrast** points out how they are different. Writers making a contrast often use one of these words: *but, however, although,* or *unlike.* Look at this example:

> The country's previous ruler had been a <u>dictator</u>. The new president, however, believed that the people should run the government.

The word *however* tells you that the new president is different from the previous ruler. The new president believes in the power of the people. A *dictator*, by contrast, is a ruler who holds complete power.
Here's another example:

> Unlike last winter, which had <u>frigid</u> weather, this winter has been very mild.

Which word signals that the sentence will express a contrast?
_____
Which word expresses a contrast to *frigid*? _____
Based on the contrast expressed in the sentence, what do you think *frigid* means?

_____

Tip

When you see an unfamiliar word, combine your knowledge of word parts (Chapters 1–4) with your knowledge of context clues. The more hints to meaning you can find, the better able you will be to figure out the word.

Words to Know: Vocabulary Lists and Activities

The various context clues we've been discussing can help you when reading different kinds of text, both in school and outside of school. Let's see how.

Reading a Nonfiction Text

The following passage is from a work of nonfiction. Read the passage and use context clues to try to figure out the meaning of the underlined words.

The Center of the Universe

For centuries, people were convinced that the earth was the center of the universe. They believed that the sun and the other planets <u>revolved</u> around the earth, while the earth remained in place. This idea of the universe was known as a <u>geocentric</u> theory, meaning "having the earth as its center" (the Greek root *geo* means "earth"). It was a <u>concept</u> based on the thinking of a great second-century astronomer named Ptolemy.

However, in the sixteenth century, a Polish astronomer named Nicolaus Copernicus saw things very differently when he <u>analyzed</u> the motion of the planets. According to Copernicus's studies, the sun, not the earth, was at the center of the universe. Furthermore, the earth moved around the sun, not the other way around. This view was known as a <u>heliocentric</u> theory, meaning "having the sun as its center" (the Greek root *helio* means "sun").

Copernicus's conclusion was <u>radically</u> different from earlier thinking. In fact, it was so <u>utterly</u> different that Copernicus kept his theory to himself for nearly thirty years. He used that time to <u>verify</u> and <u>revise</u> his work. Only when he had checked and adjusted his findings did he finally make them public.

When Copernicus published his ideas in a book in 1543, the Church condemned them as untrue. The controversy over Copernicus's revolutionary views continued for many years.

Write your definition of each word on the lines below. Then compare your definitions to those in List 21.

revolve _____

_____

geocentric _____

_____

concept _____

_____

analyze _____

_____

heliocentric _____

_____

radically _____

_____

utterly _____

_____

verify _____

_____

revise _____

_____

condemn _____

_____

List 21   Words from a Nonfiction Text

Read each word, what it means, and how it's used. Were your definitions correct?

Word	What It Means	How It's Used
revolve *(v)* ri-VOLV	to move in a path around; circle	Earth *revolves* around the sun once each year.
geocentric *(adj)* jee-oh-SEN-trik	having Earth as its center	Copernicus did not accept the *geocentric* view of the universe.
concept *(n)* KON-sept	idea or thought	Democracy is a *concept* unknown in some countries of the world.
analyze *(v)* AN-l-ize	to examine or study	Scientists *analyzed* the liquid to learn what chemicals were in it.
heliocentric *(adj)* hee-lee-oh-SEN-trik	having the sun as its center	At first, people refused to believe a *heliocentric* idea of the universe.
radically *(adv)* RAD-ik-lee	basically; completely	To get into shape, Leyora *radically* changed her eating habits.
utterly *(adv)* UHT-er-lee	absolutely; totally	I am *utterly* shocked by what she said to you!
verify *(v)* VER-uh-fie	to check for accuracy	Please *verify* your addition to make sure the answers are correct.
revise *(v)* ri-VIZE	to read over and improve or correct as needed	Paul reviewed the first draft of his report and *revised* it.
condemn *(v)* kuhn-DEM	to announce to be wrong or evil (especially to pronounce guilty in law)	The principal *condemned* the students for cheating on the test and told them they would be punished.

Own It: Develop Your Word Understanding

Share and Compare

Directions: Form a group of five people and assign each person two vocabulary words. For each of your two words, follow the steps on the next page.

1. **Compare definitions.** Compare the definition you wrote on page 142 with the definition given in the table on page 143. If necessary, make corrections to your definition. To become familiar with this new word, read the passage again with the revised definition in mind.

2. **Identify context clues.** Look again at the context clues that helped you determine the word's meaning. Referring to the list below, identify the type(s) of context clues that helped you understand the word.

Six Types of Context Clues

> descriptive details   > synonyms

> explanation or definition   > comparison

> examples   > contrast

3. **Share and compare.** Practice saying your two vocabulary words aloud. Then share these words, along with your definitions, with your group. Point out the context clues that helped you understand the words. Finally, listen as others share their results and make revisions to your definitions if necessary.

Link It: Make Word-to-World Connections

It's All in Your Head

Directions: Work with a partner to complete the activity. Here's what to do:

1. Read the headings in the table on the next page.

2. Your partner will read each vocabulary word aloud from page 143. Write it in one of the columns.

This word is completely new to me.	I have heard this word, but I've never used it.	I have used this word before.

3. Repeat step 2. This time, you read the words aloud to your partner.

4. Compare lists. Talk about when you have heard these words before and how you have used them. Read the words in the first column aloud to help them become more familiar.

Master It: Use Words in Meaningful Ways

Stargazers

Directions: Learn more about Ptolemy *or* Copernicus. When and where did the man live? Was he respected during his lifetime? Why or why not? Can you locate a drawing of what the man may have looked like?

Use your findings to prepare a report. Include paragraphs that answer the questions above or other questions you have. Use at least five vocabulary words in your work, where appropriate. Also include an image of what Ptolemy or Copernicus looked like—this could be a photocopy from a book or your own sketch based on an image in a book.

Share your report with a small group. Find out how your work is similar to and different from the work of others working on the same assignment.

Reading a Fiction Text

The following passage comes from a short story. Read the passage. As you read, use context clues to try to figure out the meaning of the underlined words.

Clashing Roommates

When Joe and his brother Tim were in middle school, they hated having to share a room. They did not have any of the same interests, and they clashed over everything, from music to sports to homework habits. Joe disliked Tim's guitar playing; the rock music irritated him.

Tim, on the other hand, didn't like how Joe was such a sports fanatic, and always watched sports loudly on their TV, especially throughout the duration of football season. It wasn't just a hobby; it was an obsession! Tim also didn't like the posters Joe wanted to put on the wall—he thought they were hideous.

Then one day their parents sat them down, and made them discuss their differences. The parents said that they were sick of Tim and Joe arguing over petty things like posters, and they wanted them to strive to get along better. Tim and Joe called a truce and agreed to compromise more. After that, they started genuinely getting along better. They still argued occasionally, but overall it was a positive transformation.

Write your definition of each word on the lines below. Then compare your definitions to those in List 22.

clash _____

_____

irritate _____

_____

fanatic _____

_____

duration _____

_____

obsession _____

_____

hideous _____

_____

petty _____

_____

strive _____

_____

truce _____

_____

transformation _____

_____

List 22   Words from a Fiction Text

Read each word, what it means, and how it's used. Were your definitions correct?

Word	What It Means	How It's Used
clash _(v)_ klash	to come into conflict	The two teams _clashed_ in a thrilling championship game.
irritate _(v)_ IR-i-tayt	to cause to feel angry or annoyed	It _irritates_ me when someone ignores what I'm saying.
fanatic _(n)_ fuh-NAT-ik	someone who is overly or unreasonably excited	Diego is such a _fanatic_ about saving electricity that he turns on the lights in only one room at a time.
duration _(n)_ doo-RAY-shuhn	the time during which something lasts	I had dinner with my parents and then went into my room and did homework for the _duration_ of the evening.
obsession _(n)_ uhb-SESH-uhn	an idea or activity that occupies too much of a person's attention	Photography became an _obsession_ for Alisha, and she took her camera everywhere.
hideous _(adj)_ HID-ee-uhs	ugly; horrible	In Didi's nightmare, she was being chased by a _hideous_ monster.
petty _(adj)_ PET-ee	having no importance or minor importance	Mom told my sister and me to stop arguing over _petty_ things like clothes.

continued

strive *(adj)* strahyv	to put forth a great deal of energy or effort	Sarah takes voice lessons and *strives* to be the best singer she can.
truce *(n)* troos	an agreement that calls the end to fighting	Jeff and Chris always fought on the basketball court until Scott convinced them to call a *truce*.
transformation *(n)* trans-fer-MAY-shuhn	change	The *transformation* of a caterpillar into a butterfly is one of nature's miracles.

Own It: Develop Your Word Understanding

Follow the Clues

Directions: In this activity, you'll learn more about the value of—and possible shortfalls of—context clues. Follow these steps.

1. Scan the passage on page 146, noting the context clues that helped you determine the meanings of vocabulary words. Then, on a sheet of paper, list the words and the context clues. If you can't identify a context clue for a word, write "no context clue."

2. In a small group, discuss context clues. To get the conversation started, answer some of these questions:

   > Which underlined words did you find context clues to?

   > Did any underlined words seem to have no context clues?

   > Did context clues seem to mislead you about the meanings of any words? If so, explain.

   > When using context clues to determine a word's meaning, what can readers do to make sure this meaning is accurate?

Tip: Using a Dictionary

When you come across an unfamiliar word, and you can't figure out its meaning from context, you may need to look it up. But dictionaries often show different forms of a word and give more than one definition. How do you know which definition is the one you need? Here are some hints.

1. First, check the part of speech. For example, if the word in question is being used as a noun (the name of a person, place, thing, or idea), then look at the noun definitions.

2. Next, check the definitions given under that part of speech and see which one makes sense in the context of what you're reading.

Imagine you looked up **clash** from the first paragraph of the passage on page 146. Which dictionary definition most accurately captures the meaning of *clash* as used in this sentence from the passage?

They did not have any of the same interests in common, and they <u>clashed</u> over everything, from music to sports to homework habits.

> **clash** *n.* **1:** a noisy sound **2:** a strong conflict
> **clash** *v.* **1:** to bang together with a loud noise **2:** to be in conflict with **3:** to not match or go well with

The passage states that the boys clashed. *Clash* is used as a verb (in the past tense) to describe an action done by a noun (the boys). So the correct definition is "clash *v.* **2:** to be in conflict with." *For a full guide to reading a dictionary entry, see Appendix A on page 220.*

Link It: Make Word-to-World Connections

Person, Place, or Thing?

Directions: Follow these steps to complete the activity.

1. Read each word in the first column of the following table.

2. In the second column, complete the sentence *This word makes me think of . . .* by writing the name of a person, place, or thing.

3. In the third column, write a sentence or two explaining the connection. Try to use the key word in your explanation.

A sample response for *clash* is completed for you.

This word . . .	. . . makes me think of. . .	Sentence
clash	the Yankees and the Red Sox.	The two teams are longtime rivals, and their fans always clash and argue with each other, too.

continued

This word . . .	. . . makes me think of . . .	Sentence
duration		
petty		
fanatic		
hideous		
strive		
truce		
transformation		
irritate		
obsession		

I am a music <u>fanatic</u>. My sister says that I'm too <u>obsessed</u> with music and that the songs I play <u>irritate</u> her. So I usually listen with headphones.

Master It: Use Words in Meaningful Ways

What Happens Next?

Directions: Reread the story on page 146. Based on what has happened so far, what do you think will happen next? Write the next part of the story using your own ideas about what characters will do, think, and say. Use as many of the vocabulary words as you can. Then participate in a storytelling festival during which you and classmates entertain one another with your tales.

Reading a Science Text

The following passage is from a science article. Read the passage and use context clues to figure out the meaning of the underlined words.

Saving Earth's Resources

We all depend on materials from the environment to feed ourselves and make our lives safe and comfortable. These materials are called <u>natural resources</u>. While many of the natural resources we use come from the land, such as wood, coal, and foods, many other resources are obtained from the sea. These <u>marine</u> resources include ocean plants and animals, minerals, and even the water itself. Natural resources also include <u>fossil fuels</u>, such as gas and oil, which we use as an energy source.

Most natural resources are not available <u>indefinitely</u>. They will eventually run out. Some are <u>renewable resources</u>, because nature can replace them as people use them. Trees and fish are examples of resources that nature can <u>replenish</u> over time. Other materials are known as <u>nonrenewable resources</u>. Unlike renewable resources, nonrenewable resources cannot be replaced. Substances that form over millions of years, such as coal or oil, or that are available in limited amounts in nature, such as copper or gold, are nonrenewable resources.

It's important to wisely manage and safeguard our natural resources to make sure that they will be available far into the future. The careful management and protection of natural resources and the environment in which they are found is called <u>conservation</u>.

The nations of the world do not all view the need for conservation from the same <u>perspective</u>. Their individual commitment to looking after our environment varies. For example, some countries declare large areas of land to be protected. Others do not see it as a <u>grave</u> issue and do not set aside any protected areas. Organizations such as the World Wildlife Fund and Greenpeace promote conservation around the world.

Write your definition of each word on the lines below. Then compare your definitions to those in List 23.

natural resources _____

_____

marine _____

_____

fossil fuels _____

_____

indefinitely _____

_____

renewable resources _____

_____

replenish _____

_____

nonrenewable resources _____

_____

conservation _____

_____

perspective _____

_____

grave _____

_____

List 23   Words from a Science Text

Read each word, what it means, and how it's used. Were your definitions correct?

Word	What It Means	How It's Used
natural resources *(n)* NACH-er-uhl REE-sawrs-ez	materials from nature that people use or eat	Clean water is one of our most precious *natural resources*.
marine *(adj)* muh-REEN	relating to the sea	Divers explore the ocean, studying *marine* life.
fossil fuels *(n)* FOS-uhl FEW-uhlz	fuels such as coal, gas, and oil used as an energy source	Burning *fossil fuels* contributes to air pollution.
indefinitely *(adv)* in-DEF-uh-nit-lee	without limit; endlessly	The runner set a fast pace at the start of the race, but he couldn't keep it up *indefinitely*.
renewable resources *(n)* ri-NOO-a-BUHL REE-sawrs-ez	natural resources that nature can replace as they are used	The wood we use to construct houses is a *renewable resource*.
replenish *(v)* ri-PLEN-ish	to fill up again or stock up	I'm going to Stop & Shop with my mom after school to *replenish* our supply of breakfast cereal.
nonrenewable resources *(n)* NON-ri-NOO-a-buhl REE-sawrs-ez	natural resources that cannot be replaced once used	Metals like iron and silver are *nonrenewable resources*.

continued

conservation *(n)* kon-ser-VAY-shuhn	careful management and protection of natural resources and the environment	As part of the nation's *conservation* effort, drivers are urged to save gas by driving less.
perspective *(n)* per-SPEK-tiv	a point of view	I never thought of it that way; you see things from a different *perspective* than I do.
grave *(adj)* greyv	very serious	Cheating on that test was a *grave* mistake that will prevent you from getting an A in this course.

Own It: Develop Your Word Understanding

Science Term Organizers

Directions: Use the following six graphic organizers to become more familiar with the science terms in the word list. Work with a partner to complete the steps.

1. Review the words and their definitions in the table above and on the previous page. With your partner, form a definition in your own words for the word at the top of each organizer. Write it in the box on the left.

2. In the box on the right, give examples that help clarify the meaning of the key word.

3. In the bottom section, answer the question.

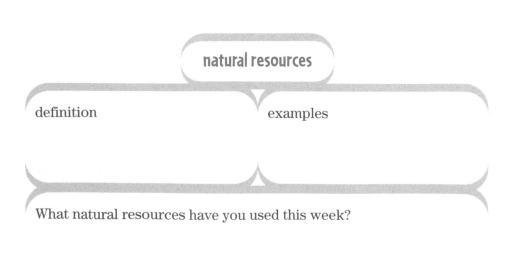

natural resources

definition

examples

What natural resources have you used this week?

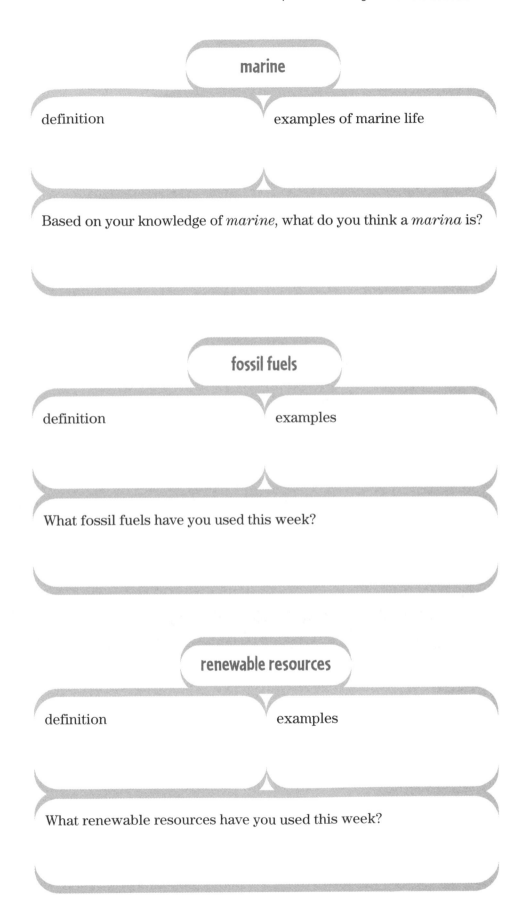

marine

definition

examples of marine life

Based on your knowledge of *marine*, what do you think a *marina* is?

fossil fuels

definition

examples

What fossil fuels have you used this week?

renewable resources

definition

examples

What renewable resources have you used this week?

nonrenewable resources

| definition | examples |

What nonrenewable resources have you used this week?

conservation

| definition | examples |

What is one conservation effort that you actively support?

Link It: Make Word-to-World Connections

Now and Later

Directions: In this activity, you'll think about words and terms you're learning now, and how these words may come in handy later. Pair up with a classmate and follow these steps:

1. One of you reads the first entry in the vocabulary list. Together, make sure that you understand its meaning.

2. On a sheet of paper, write the term. Then write an example of when or how you might use it in the future.

3. Repeat steps 1 and 2 for each word or term in List 23.

4. In a class discussion, share some of your results. Point out any words that you don't see yourself using in the future—and prepare to be surprised and informed by how others *do* plan to use the words!

Master It: Use Words in Meaningful Ways

Did You Know?

Directions: In this activity, you will choose one vocabulary word or term to explore further. Then you'll share a few facts about this word with your classmates. Follow these steps:

1. Review the list of vocabulary words and their meanings. Choose one of the science terms from 154–156 that seems most interesting to you.

2. Find **two or three** facts about the word that you can share with your class. For instance, what are some types of *marine* life that are endangered? What is the government doing to promote the *conservation* of resources? Useful sources of information include nonfiction books, encyclopedias, magazine articles, and documentaries.

3. Write a few sentences stating two or three facts about the vocabulary word. Here are some phrases that you could use to begin the sentences:

   > Did you know that . . .

   > A surprising fact about (*vocabulary word*) is . . .

   > A question I had about (*vocabulary word*) was . . .

4. Practice reading your sentences aloud. Then read your sentences to your classmates.

Reading a History Text

The following passage comes from a history textbook. Read the passage. As you read, use context clues to try to figure out the meaning of the underlined words.

The Renaissance Period

The <u>Renaissance</u> was a period in history when European artists and writers became interested again in <u>classical</u> culture. The French word *Renaissance* means "rebirth"—in this case, the rebirth of interest in the ancient Greek and Roman world. The Renaissance lasted from about 1300 to 1600.

The Renaissance began in Italy. Later it spread to Spain, France, England, the Netherlands (Holland), and other countries of Western Europe. Italy was in the <u>forefront</u> of the movement, leading the way as trade increased and towns grew into cities. The merchants and bankers who had become wealthy from trade helped support the arts. For example, the Medici, a rich family of bankers in Florence, Italy, <u>financed</u> famous works of art and <u>architecture</u>, or building design.

People of the Renaissance developed new ways of viewing the world. They were especially <u>engaged</u> in the art and literature of the ancient Greeks and Romans. They were also more interested in <u>secular</u>, or worldly, matters. In this way they differed from <u>medieval</u> thinkers. During the Middle Ages (about 500–1500), people paid more attention to religious subjects. Renaissance thinkers <u>acquired</u> a fresh outlook. They celebrated life and showed interest in <u>humanism</u>. This was the idea that each person was unique, one of a kind, and had great worth in the world.

Write your definition of each word on the lines below. Then compare your definitions to those in List 24.

Renaissance _____

_____

classical _____

_____

forefront _____

_____

finance _____

_____

architecture _____

_____

engaged _____

_____

secular _____

_____

medieval _____

_____

acquire _____

_____

humanism _____

_____

List 24   Words from a History Text

Read each word, what it means, and how it's used. Were your definitions correct?

Word	What It Means	How It's Used
Renaissance _(n)_ ren-uh-SAHNS	historical period during which there was new interest in ancient Greek and Roman culture	The _Renaissance_ started in Italy and spread to other parts of Europe.
classical _(adj)_ KLAS-i-kuhl	relating to the art, literature, and culture of ancient Greece and Rome	Reading the works of famous writers of ancient Greece is part of _classical_ studies.
forefront _(n)_ FAWR-fruhnt	position of greatest importance or activity; leading position	This university is at the _forefront_ of medical research.
finance _(v)_ fi-NANS	to provide money for	Emma's parents helped to _finance_ her college education.
architecture _(n)_ AHR-ki-tek-cher	the art or science of designing and constructing buildings	Modern _architecture_ makes use of steel and glass.
engaged _(adj)_ en-GAYJD	involved or interested in	The students were quietly _engaged_ in their work.
secular _(adj)_ SEK-yuh-ler	relating to worldly things; not religious	In a _secular_ government, the rulers are not religious leaders.

continued

medieval *(adj)* mee-dee-EE-vuhl	of the Middle Ages	In *medieval* times, knights served their king.
acquire *(v)* uh-KWY-r	to come to have; get	Over the years, Dad has *acquired* considerable skill in woodworking.
humanism *(n)* HYOO-muh-niz-uhm	the idea that each person is special and has great worth in the world	People who believe in *humanism* recognize the value of each person.

Own It: Develop Your Word Understanding

Game Show

Directions: In this activity, you will be part of a game show team. When your team is "onstage" (in front of the class), the rest of the class will be your audience. Here's how the game show works:

1. Assemble your team onstage. Choose one or two hosts, while the rest of you line up as contestants.

2. The host reads the definition of a vocabulary word. This is the *answer* to a question. If you know the *question*, raise your hand.

3. The host calls on the first person to raise a hand. This person must ask the *question* that matches the host's answer. For instance, if the host read, "Of the Middle Ages," then the correct question is, "What is medieval?"

4. Each correct *question* wins a point. The game is over when each definition has been matched to the correct question. Finally, add up contestants' points to see who won.

Link It: Make Word-to-World Connections

New Contexts

Directions: When you read the passage on pages 157–8, you read each vocabulary word in the context of that passage. In this activity, you'll choose a vocabulary word and put it into a different context. Grab a partner and follow these steps.

1. Toss around ideas of how you could put vocabulary words into different contexts. For instance, you could use *classical* in a

description of music. You could use *medieval* to explain the setting of a video game. You could also use a word in a graphic novel or comic strip.

2. Based on your ideas in step 1, choose the word you would most like to work with.

3. Use your creativity to bring the word to life in its new context. A basic plan, for instance, is to write a paragraph. For added appeal, use graphics, music, costumes, or objects along with your written or spoken words.

4. Present your word in its new context to the class.

If I could <u>acquire</u> enough money to <u>finance</u> a guitar, that might help me meet girls... I'm sure they'd find my playing to be <u>engaging</u>...

Master It: Use Words in Meaningful Ways

Seek and Find

Directions: In this activity, you'll choose a question from the list on the next page and write a short report to answer the question. To answer the question, you'll need to do a little research. You may want to ask a librarian or teacher to recommend a source on your chosen topic.

After you research and write your report, share it with a small group in class.

Research Questions

1. What does the term "*Renaissance* man" mean? Could you use it to describe a modern person?

2. Who are some *classical* Greek and Roman writers and what did they write?

3. Who was one of the artists at the *forefront* of the Italian Renaissance? What type of work did this artist create?

4. Why did some Renaissance artists need someone to *finance* them? Give an example of an artist who was *financed* by a patron.

5. What did Renaissance *architecture* look like?

6. Give an example of religious art and then contrast it to an example of *secular* art.

7. What are some elements of the *medieval* period that were rejected during the *Renaissance*?

8. A few *humanist* thinkers of the Renaissance are Desiderius Erasmus, Sir Thomas More, Francesco Petrarch, and Francis Bacon. What are some key facts about one of these men?

Wrapping Up: Review What You've Learned

Here's a brief summary of what you've studied in this chapter.

> When you come upon an unfamiliar word, context clues can help you figure out the meaning of the word.

> **Context** means the words or sentences that come before and after a particular word.

> Sometimes you need very little context to figure out a word's meaning. Other times, you may have to consider a whole paragraph.

> There are various kinds of context clues, including

>> descriptive details

>> explanation or definition

>> examples

>> synonyms

>> comparison

>> contrast

> Combining your knowledge of word parts with your knowledge of context clues can make it easier to figure out the meaning of unfamiliar words.

Flaunt It: Show Your Word Understanding

In the following exercises, you'll demonstrate your understanding of each vocabulary word. You will use vocabulary words, or forms of the words, to complete sentences and to write sentences of your own.

A **Sentence Completion**

Directions: Circle the letter of the pair of words or terms that best complete each sentence.

1. _____ take millions of years to form, and Earth's supply is being used faster than new stores can form. Therefore, they are considered to be _____.

   a. Renewable resources, nonrenewable resources

   b. Natural resources, fossil fuels

   c. Fossil fuels, nonrenewable resources

   d. Fossil fuels, indefinite

2. The _____ was a time of rich artistic production. Some of the amazing _____ of the time can still be seen today in cathedrals and other buildings.

   a. Renaissance, architecture

   b. medieval, architecture

   c. forefront, humanism

   d. classical, finance

3. My brother's constant presence in my room was beginning to _____ me, so I told him he was banned from my room for the _____ of the year.

   a. clash, forefront

   b. irritate, duration

   c. irritate, forefront

   d. clash, transformation

4. One of Ricardo's best qualities is his deep, _____ voice. Whenever he speaks, people feel _____ drawn to what he is saying.

   a. fanatic, indefinitely

   b. hideous, indefinitely

   c. secular, gravely

   d. engaging, utterly

5. _____ of energy is important at my house. In fact, you could say that I am a _____ about turning off lights, radios, televisions, and other devices the instant that someone is finished using them.

   a. Transformation, fanatic

   b. Transformation, natural resource

   c. Conservation, renewable resource

   d. Conservation, fanatic

B   Word Bank

Directions: Choose a word from the box to complete each sentence. Write the word on the line provided. Each word may be used only once.

> analyzing   hideous   marine   concept   acquire
> finance   clashed   revise   radically   transformation

When Mom told me that she would **(6)** _____ a makeover of my bedroom, I was thrilled. I wanted to **(7)**_____ lots of cool posters and artwork to hang on my walls.

   Then Mom gave me my remodeling money: fifty dollars. What? How could I remake this **(8)**_____ room with only fifty dollars? I would have to **(9)**_____ my grand plans.

   After **(10)**_____ my options, I decided to spend a chunk of my budget on paint. A bold, bright color would **(11)**_____ change the look of the room. I bought ocean-blue paint and coated the walls. To extend the **(12)**_____ theme, I arranged my collection of seashells on a shelf. I could almost smell the salty sea air!

   I liked the **(13)**_____ of an open, spacious room, so I took down the heavy, dark curtains. I replaced them with billowy curtains the color of clouds. Since my red bedspread **(14)**_____ with the blue-and-white color scheme, I bought a new one with beach umbrellas printed on it. The **(15)**_____ of my room was complete, and I had created a "seaside" paradise.

 **Writing**

Directions: Follow the directions to write sentences using vocabulary words, or forms of the words. Write your sentences on a separate sheet of paper.

16. Use *hideous* in a description of a clothing item or accessory you would never wear.

17. Use *verify* to describe a time you checked to see if you were right about something.

18. Use *radically* to describe a change you underwent or a change you observed in someone else (a real person or someone in a movie, book, or TV show).

19. Use *marine* to tell about an idea for a movie.

20. Use *medieval* to tell about an idea for an electronic game.

Chapter Extension Activities

Activities à la Carte: Extend Your Word Knowledge

The activities on this page are presented à la carte, like items on a restaurant menu, meaning that you can choose from a variety of options. Your teacher may assign an activity or let you pick the one that tempts your appetite. If time allows, you might do more than one activity. All of the activities feature the same ingredient: **context clues**. Dig in!

Track Five

For the next five days, keep track of new words you learn by studying context clues. Try to collect examples from all types of reading that you do—school assignments, magazines, fiction, messages from friends, and so on. After five days, you'll have a concrete measure of how much your literacy has increased.

Talk with Your Mouth Full

The next time you eat lunch with your friends, talk with your mouth full! Why? To study the value of context when it comes to understanding everything you hear. As converse, notice times when you are able to figure out what your friend meant by a garbled a word. Chances are, this won't be the first time you use context to understand a friend's words completely!

Sling Some Slang

Many slang words carry meaning based on how they are used in a sentence—based on context, in other words. Brainstorm a list of slang words and terms that you and your friends use. Choose five of them that could have different meanings, depending on how they are used. Then write sentences showing at least two uses of each word or term. (Alternative: You can also pick words that had different meanings years ago. Ask your parents, grandparents, or other older relatives for words that were used differently when they were young.)

Multiple-Meaning You

As you know, multiple-meaning words carry different meanings, depending on context. Have you ever thought of yourself as a multiple-meaning person? How does your behavior, dress, and conversation change based on whom you are around? Analyze at least two contexts that you are in regularly—perhaps home and school. List ways you behave, dress, or talk differently in each context.

 ## It's Greek to Me

If you have studied a second language, then you know what it's like to struggle to translate a sentence. You start with words you know and use those words as clues to the meanings of unfamiliar words. With a language-study group or your class, share some examples of how you learned new words using context clues.

Clue Review

Using context clues to determine word meaning can serve you well long after this lesson is over. With this in mind, create a poster-sized cheat sheet that lists and explains the types of context clues taught in this lesson. Use colorful paint or paper to make the poster eye-catching. Hang this clue review in your classroom or near a table where you normally do homework.

Thinking About Different Word Meanings

8

In a sense, words are like tools. As a writer, you choose the right tools to do the job. As a reader, you respond to how authors use words to create meaning. With experience in reading and writing, you gain greater skill in using the tools of the trade: words.

This chapter offers you three types of tools to add to your toolbox. You'll learn about words with more than one meaning, literal and figurative uses of words, and descriptive words with specific meanings. You may recognize some of these words. Others will be new discoveries.

Objectives

In this chapter, you will learn

> Words that have more than one meaning
> Words that can be used literally or figuratively (in an expression)
> Words that have very specific meanings

Sneak Peek: Preview the Lesson

Tools of the Trade

Take a look at the word list on the next page, featuring some of the words you'll learn in this chapter. Which ones are familiar? Which ones are new to you? Which words seem so "foreign" that you can't imagine ever using them? Sort the words into categories, based on your responses. (You can put a word in more than one category.) After you complete the chapter, come back to this page and evaluate your progress in adding "tools" to your vocabulary toolbox!

Word List

element	suspend	sly	sleek
fuse	recluse	shabby	courteous
positive	stale	lanky	romantic

I've used this word before.	I have not used this word.	I can't imagine ever using this word.

Vocabulary Mini-Lesson: Understanding Words with More than One Meaning

When you look up a word in a dictionary, you often find that the word has more than one meaning. Consider the word *note*, for example. How many meanings of this word can you think of? Compare the following sentences.

Emily wrote me a thank-you <u>note</u>.

The <u>note</u> at the bottom of the page explained the word's meaning.

Your excellent grades are worthy of <u>note</u>.

The singer kept practicing until she could hit the high <u>note</u>.

There was a <u>note</u> of sadness in his voice.

And these are just some of the *noun* meanings! There are other noun meanings, as well as several *verb* meanings.

While most words don't have as many meanings as *note* does, you may be surprised by how many words do have more than one meaning. You may also be surprised to find that many familiar words have less familiar additional meanings. For example, when you hear the word *skate*, you probably think of ice skates or roller skates. But did you know that a skate is also a kind of fish?

> ### Tip
> Words with the same spelling but different meanings are often referred to as *homographs*. (*homo-* = same; *graph* = written)

Words to Know: Vocabulary Lists and Activities

In this section, you'll study two lists of words with more than one meaning.

List 25   Words with Multiple Meanings

Read each word, its two or three possible meanings, and the sample sentences.

Word	What It Means	How It's Used
conduct *(v)* kuhn-DUHKT	**1.** to show the way; lead	**1.** The guide *conducted* a tour of the building.
	2. to direct the performance of	**2.** Our music teacher *conducted* the orchestra.
	3. to direct or manage; carry out	**3.** Detectives *conducted* an investigation of the crime scene.
deposit *(v)* di-POZ-it	**1.** to place for safekeeping	**1.** Jake went to the bank to *deposit* the money he had earned.
	2. to put down; leave behind	**2.** Flood waters *deposited* mud in the streets.
element *(n)* EL-uh-muhnt	**1.** one of the basic substances from which all matter is made up	**1.** Oxygen and hydrogen are the chemical *elements* that form water.
	2. a part or quality	**2.** This short story has an *element* of surprise.

continued

fuse *(n)* fyooz	1. a cord, wick, or other device used to set off an explosive charge	1. To protect themselves from the blast, the miners took cover when the *fuse* was lit.
	2. a safety device placed in an electric circuit to prevent dangerous overload	2. Plugging in too many electrical appliances may blow a *fuse*.
issue *(n)* ISH-oo	1. a topic to be considered or discussed	1. The two candidates debated the *issue* of taxes.
	2. something sent out or published	2. Have you read the latest *issue* of *Sports Illustrated*?

Own It: Develop Your Word Understanding

Multiple-Meaning Mixer

Directions: In this activity, you will be given a vocabulary word *or* a definition. Your job is to find a classmate who has the corresponding vocabulary word or definition. Here's how the activity works:

1. Your teacher will fill a box with index cards. Each card will have either a vocabulary word or a definition written on it.

2. Take one card from the box.

3. Move around the classroom to find the person who has the word or definition that corresponds to what's written on your card. Since each word has more than one meaning, you'll form a group of three or four people.

4. With your group, review the multiple meanings of your word. Practice explaining the word's meanings in your own words rather than repeating the definitions in the book. Then write sentences that demonstrate the different meanings. Write one sentence for each meaning.

5. In a class discussion, take turns with members of your group to explain your word's multiple meanings and read your sentences aloud.

Link It: Make Word-to-World Connections

Me, Myself, and I

Directions: In this activity, you'll choose *one* meaning of five vocabulary words to use in describing yourself or your world. Follow these steps:

1. The vocabulary words are listed below. Decide which meaning of each word best connects to your life—to an experience you've had, for instance, or to a description of yourself or your neighborhood.

2. In the space beside each key word, explain which meaning of the word best connects to you or your life, and why.

3. Share some of your results with the class.

Word	Meaning That Best Connects to Me and My World
conduct	
deposit	
element	
fuse	
issue	

Master It: Use Words in Meaningful Ways

Here's How It Works

Directions: In this activity, you'll choose one vocabulary word to research and write about. Follow these steps:

1. Review the list of vocabulary words and their meanings on pages 171–172. As you do so, let your curiosity go wild, asking questions about each word. For example, how does someone *conduct* an orchestra? How can someone my age open a bank account and *deposit* money?

2. Choose one of the questions you asked in step 1 and go find answers. Useful sources of information are interviews, how-to books, Web sites recommended by a teacher or librarian, and other nonfiction sources.

3. Write an informative report about the question you researched. Your teacher may ask you to read your report aloud. He or she may also collect the reports in a folder so that students can read them when they have spare time.

List 26 Words with Multiple Meanings

Here is a second list of words with more than one meaning. Read each word, its two or three possible meanings, and the sample sentences.

Word	What It Means	How It's Used
operation *(n)* op-uh-RAY-shuhn	1. a medical procedure done to the body for the purpose of restoring health	1. Doctors said that Joe would need an *operation* to repair his knee.
	2. way of working	2. The machine was so complicated that few people understood its *operation*.
	3. action by military or government forces	3. Soldiers carried out the secret *operation* in hopes of preventing a war.
positive *(adj)* POZ-i-tiv	1. not open to question; certain	1. Results of the study offer *positive* proof that this drug cures the disease.
	2. indicating that someone approves, agrees, or accepts	2. The teacher wrote many *positive* comments on Terry's paper.

continued

reference *(n)* REF-er-enss	1. the directing of attention to	1. The mayor's speech contained many *references* to the city's traffic problems.
	2. source of information	2. Students often use an encyclopedia as a *reference* when they write reports.
	3. a person who can provide information about or a recommendation for another	3. On her application for a summer job, Katrina listed her teacher as a *reference*.
register *(v)* REJ-uh-ster	1. to enter one's name in a record	1. Citizens must *register* in order to vote in the election.
	2. to indicate; show	2. The thermometer *registered* a record high temperature.
suspend *(v)* suh-SPEND	1. to cause to stop temporarily	1. The train station is going to *suspend* service during the storm. We will *suspend* the ornament on the tree.
	2. to hold in place from above; hang	2. The ornament was *suspended* by a thin wire.

Own It: Develop Your Word Understanding

Monkey See

Directions: In this activity, you'll take a vocabulary word from List 26 and demonstrate one of its definitions. How? By giving your classmates something to *see* as a learning aid. Grab a partner and follow these steps:

1. Review the vocabulary words and their definitions. Toss around ideas for how you could *show* classmates what words mean. For example, to remember one meaning of *operation*, you could show classmates the children's game Operation. G.I. Joe figures could demonstrate another meaning of *operation*. To demonstrate one meaning of *suspend*, you could hold up a pendant *suspended* on a chain.

2. Choose one word and one definition for your project. Find or create something to *show* that teaches one meaning of the word.

3. Teach your word and the meaning to your class by showing your learning aid and explaining the word's meaning.

Link It: Make Word-to-World Connections

Give It a Day

Directions: For one day, watch for ways the vocabulary words relate to your world. Keep a notebook handy and jot down every idea that day. For instance, you may see a news story about troop *operations*, your sister may *register* for an art class, or a friend may say he is *positive* that someone is planning a surprise party for him.

Report back to your class. Tell them how many examples you collected and read a few aloud. Tell them whether you noticed examples for every word, or if a word didn't show up in your world that day. Some vocabulary words have more meanings than are listed in the table. If you used one of these additional meanings, be sure to point that out.

The latest issue of our school newspaper talks about discipline issues. Should the students who <u>suspended</u> a bucket of water from the ceiling in the hallway be <u>suspended</u> from school?

Master It: Use Words in Meaningful Ways

Tell Me About It

Directions: Choose one of the following five topics. Gather information on the topic and tell your class about it in an oral report.

> Explain the *operation* of a device or piece of equipment.

> Explain what *positive* reinforcement is.

> Explain various *reference* sources that students may use.

> Explain how to *register* for an extracurricular activity.

> Explain what *suspended* animation is.

Get approval to explain a topic that you develop. Be sure that your topic uses a vocabulary word!

Vocabulary Mini-Lesson: Understanding Literal and Figurative Uses of Words

Most of the time, we use words according to their *literal* meaning, or dictionary definition. However, we can also use words *figuratively*, in creative ways. With figurative language, a writer creates a striking mental image or makes an idea memorable. When you read figurative language, you must *interpret* the meaning instead of just defining the words. Take a look at these examples.

Literal: Dr. Frankenstein created a frightening <u>monster</u> in his laboratory.
(The monster is literal. It is actually there in the laboratory.)

Figurative: Eric was a <u>monster</u> who teased and frightened younger boys.
(Eric is not actually a monster. He is a boy whose behavior makes him seem like a monster.)

As you can see, when you use a word literally, you mean exactly what you say. When you use a word figuratively, you are expressing an idea creatively, not literally.

Here is another example of literal and figurative uses of a word.

Literal: The dog was <u>starving</u> because it hadn't been fed in many days.
(The dog is actually starving to death.)

Figurative: I am <u>starving</u>! When is lunch?
(The speaker is extremely hungry. The speaker is *not* actually dying from lack of food.)

When you read sentences that use words figuratively, remember this: The writer is expressing an idea creatively. You must interpret the figurative language in order to understand the word's use in the sentence. The table that follows will help you recognize ways words are used figuratively.

Type of Figurative Language	Explanation	Example
metaphor	a comparison of two things that says one thing *is* the other thing	The rumbling volcano was a <u>sleeping dragon</u> ready to wake up and breathe fire.
simile	a comparison that uses a word such as *like* or *as*	This steak is tough as <u>leather</u>.
hyperbole	exaggeration to create an effect or to make a point	Taylor has a <u>million</u> pairs of shoes.
personification	giving human qualities, such as thoughts or speech, to animals or nonliving things	Leaves <u>danced</u> in the treetops.
irony	a statement of the opposite of what is meant or expected	That plastic ring is a real <u>treasure</u>.

When you see words used figuratively, as in the examples above, ask, "What image is the writer creating with this word?" or "What point is the writer making with this word?" These questions will help you understand the figurative use of a word.

W ords to Know: Vocabulary Lists and Activities

In the following section, you'll study two lists of words that are used literally and figuratively.

List 27 Words Used Literally and Figuratively

Read each word, what it means, and how it's used both literally and figuratively. Note the kind of figurative language in each example.

Word	What It Means	How It's Used
toxic *(adj)* TOK-sick	containing poison	**literal:** He sprayed the mousetrap with a solution that is very *toxic* to rodents. **metaphor:** According to gossip columns, that celebrity is *toxic* and is always being nasty to people or starting arguments. (The celebrity is not literally made of poison, but she has a personality that's harmful.)
sly *(adj)* slahy	clever and sneaky	**literal:** The *sly* boy tricked his friend into mowing the lawn for him. **simile:** That boy is as *sly* as a fox. (Comparing the boy's slyness to that of a fox is a creative way of saying the boy is clever and sneaky.)
recluse *(n)* REK-loos	someone who leads a solitary life	**literal:** I read a story about a king who was a *recluse* who stayed in his castle for five years. **hyperbole:** During finals, he became a *recluse*; he studied at his desk all weekend and only left his room for meals. (This is an exaggerated way of saying that he is spending a lot of time studying on his own, instead of being social. It's an exaggeration because he's not completely alone, and it's not for a long period of time.)
forlorn *(adj)* fawr-LAWRN	sad and lonely	**literal:** Jana feels *forlorn* because all her friends are out of town this week. **personification:** A *forlorn* plant sat on the dusty windowsill. (A plant doesn't have emotions, so it can't actually feel forlorn.)
civilized *(adj)* SIV-uh-lahyzd	characterized by good taste, manners, and refinement	**literal:** My aunt is very *civilized* and comments on people's dinner-table manners. **irony:** I like how you're eating spaghetti with your bare hands—how *civilized* of you. (The speaker is being sarcastic and implying the person is not civilized—is not showing manners.)

Own It: Develop Your Word Understanding

Divide and Conquer

Directions: Work with a partner to complete the activity. Here's what to do:

1. Divide the ten sentences between you.
2. Read each of your sentences and decide if the underlined word is used literally or figuratively. Write *L* or *F* next to the sentence to indicate your answer.
3. Share your results with your partner and explain your answers.
4. In a class discussion, talk about sentences that were challenging or confusing. Revise your answers as necessary.

_____ **1.** He started that rumor with a really <u>toxic</u> e-mail.

_____ **2.** I've never met my neighbor; she's a <u>recluse</u> and never leaves the house.

_____ **3.** Only a <u>sly</u> person could have followed me, unnoticed, to my hideout.

_____ **4.** A <u>forlorn</u> baby chick wandered aimlessly, far from its mother.

_____ **5.** As the argument progressed, the two former friends started calling each other names and throwing things; it was a <u>civilized</u> discussion indeed.

_____ **6.** Some cleaning solutions are <u>toxic</u> if accidentally swallowed.

_____ **7.** When my best friend suddenly moved away, I was <u>forlorn</u> for weeks.

_____ **8.** We got dressed up and attended a very <u>civilized</u> social gathering at a five-star restaurant downtown.

_____ **9.** I am going to be a <u>recluse</u> for the rest of my life; I can't go out in public with this zit on my nose!

_____ **10.** The burglar was as <u>sly</u> as a rat seeking cheese.

Link It: Make Word-to-World Connections

Figurative Trading Cards

Directions: In this activity, you'll use vocabulary words figuratively to create trading cards. Here's what to do:

1. Gather supplies. You need five index cards, pens, paints, photos, and any other art supplies you want to use.
2. On each card, print one vocabulary word from List 27.

3. On each card, draw or glue an image that corresponds to a figurative use of the word. For instance, on the *forlorn* card you could draw a picture of an empty house. To interpret this card, you would say that the house is forlorn because no one lives there anymore. Be sure to sign your name somewhere on each card.

4. In class, take part in a Figurative Trading Card Festival. Move around the room, showing your cards to others. You may need to interpret some cards for some people. Trade your cards for other cards that capture your interest.

Master It: Use Words in Meaningful Ways

Literal or Figurative?

Directions: In this activity, you'll practice using words literally and figuratively. Follow these steps:

1. Write five sentences, each one using a different vocabulary word. Use some vocabulary words literally and use others figuratively. These sentences may tell something about yourself, your neighborhood, or something else from your world. (Use the Figurative Trading Card activity on page 180 for inspiration.)

2. Trade sentences with a classmate. Read each sentence, and decide whether the vocabulary word is used literally or figuratively. Write L or F above the word to show your opinion.

3. Share the results with your partner and talk about any sentences that were challenging.

List 28   Words Used Literally and Figuratively

Here is the second list of words used literally and figuratively. Read each word, what it means, and how it's used. Note the kind of figurative language in each example.

Word	What It Means	How It's Used
stale *(adj)* steyl	dry and tasteless as a result of having been kept too long	**literal:** This bread was fresh last week, but now it's *stale*. **metaphor:** The comedian's jokes were *stale*, boring the audience. (The jokes were old or unoriginal.)

continued

whimper (v) HWIM-per	to make a low cry or sound that expresses displeasure	**literal:** The child *whimpered* in fear during the thunderstorm. **simile:** Greta *whimpered* like a puppy when she spilled juice on her favorite sweater. (Comparing Greta's cries to those of a puppy suggests she is helpless or weak.)
epic (n) EP-ik	a long narrative that tells about someone's heroic deeds, or something in history that is worthy of such a narrative	**literal:** The *Odyssey* is an *epic* poem about the tales of a character named Odysseus. **hyperbole:** Natalie told me the *epic* tale of her weekend. (Calling it an epic tale is an exaggeration.)
lurk (v) lurk	to lie hidden but waiting, especially for evil purposes	**literal:** The cougar *lurked* near the deer, hungry for its next meal. **personification:** Thorny bushes *lurked* along the dark path. (Bushes can't have evil purposes, like a person, but the personification creates a vivid image.)
adept (adj) uh-DEPT	being highly trained or skilled, or having expertise	**literal:** She is a really *adept* skater; she always scores well at competitions. **irony:** Yeah, I can tell you're really *adept* at baking—your brownies taste like flavorless bricks! (The speaker is using irony to point out that the person is *not adept*.)

Own It: Develop Your Word Understanding

Two Sides of the Coin

Directions: Each vocabulary word is like a coin with a literal side and a figurative side. You have one coin but more than one way to "spend" it. To become familiar with literal and figurative uses of each word, complete the five sets of coins on the next two pages. Follow these steps.

1. On the Literal side of the coin, write a sentence that uses the word literally. For example, *A thief <u>lurked</u> near the jewelry store.*

2. On the Figurative side of the coin, write a sentence that uses the word figuratively. For example, *I woke at midnight to see shadows <u>lurking</u> around my bed.*

3. In a class discussion, share some of your work.

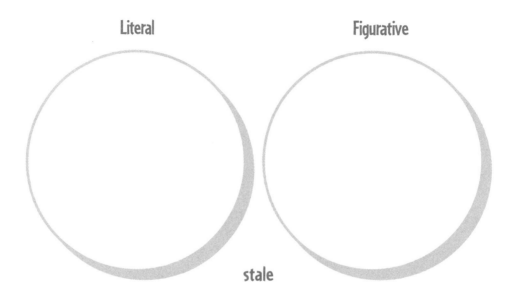

stale

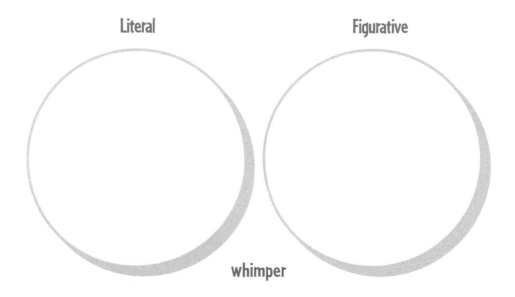

whimper

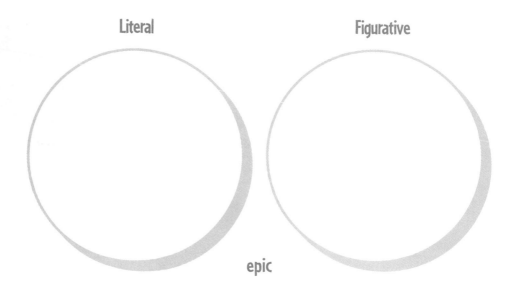

Literal

Figurative

epic

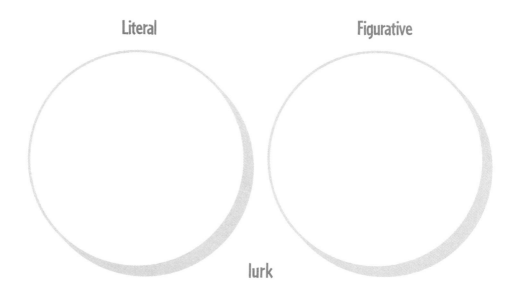

Literal

Figurative

lurk

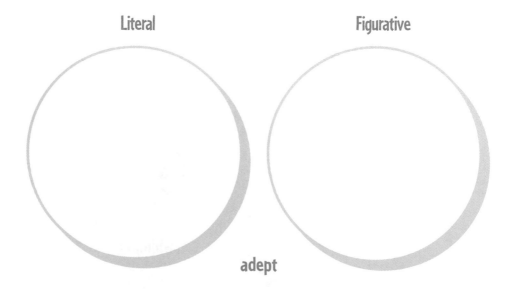

Literal

Figurative

adept

Link It: Make Word-to-World Connections

Spin the Bottle

Directions: In this activity, you'll practice using words literally and figuratively. First, your teacher will place you in small groups and give each group an empty plastic bottle. Then follow these steps:

1. Place the bottle on a desk in the center of your group. One of you spins the bottle. Wait for the bottle to stop, pointing at someone. Then ask this person, "Literal or figurative?" When the person chooses, give him or her a vocabulary word.

2. The person makes up a sentence that uses the vocabulary word literally or figuratively, depending on the choice made.

3. This person becomes the new bottle spinner, and the process repeats. If you run out of vocabulary words, use words from List 27 (page 179).

Okay, I admit the joke I told at lunch was a little <u>stale</u>, but that didn't mean my buddy had to blow his straw wrapper at me... that wasn't very civilized of him!

Master It: Use Words in Meaningful Ways

Five-Minute Mastery

Directions: In this activity, you'll write very quickly for five minutes about **one** vocabulary word. Here's how the activity works:

1. Choose one vocabulary word from List 28.

2. Get out a sheet of paper, and set a timer for five minutes. (Your teacher may watch the time for you.) Begin by writing the first thought in your head about the vocabulary word. This thought could be a definition, a sentence using the word, a

memory inspired by the word, or any other thought. There is no "wrong" thing to write.

3. Keep writing. Don't stop! Use the word literally. Use it figuratively. Write questions, lines of poetry, descriptions, statements, phrases, and anything else that comes to mind. Let one thought lead into the next.

4. After five minutes, stop writing.

5. Read what you wrote. Indulge in feelings of satisfaction and pride in your five-minute mastery of the vocabulary word.

Vocabulary Mini-Lesson: Using Descriptive Words with Specific Meanings

As writers and speakers, we're always using words to describe people, places, and things. For example:

I saw a good movie last night.

Mr. Greene works in a big office building.

Maria is a nice girl.

However, when you hear descriptions like these, the best you can do is guess at their meaning.

What made it a "good" movie? Was it funny? Exciting?

In what way is Mr. Greene's building "big"? Is it huge, like a skyscraper? Or does it simply contain many offices?

What makes Maria a "nice" girl? Is she generous? Friendly?

Describing words like *good*, *big*, and *nice* give only a general idea of meaning. They are not precise (exact). By using specific descriptive words when you write and speak, you can get your ideas across more clearly. Like figurative language, descriptive words will help your reader or listener get a clear picture of what you mean.

Words to Know: Vocabulary Lists and Activities

In the following section, you'll study a list of words that describe physical features and appearances, and a list of words that describe behavior and actions.

List 29   Words That Describe Physical Features and Appearance

Study these ten sharp, descriptive words (all adjectives). Read each word, what it means, and how it's used. As you read each sample sentence, try to think of your own examples of how you would use the word.

Word	What It Means	How It's Used
fragrant *(adj)* FRAY-gruhnt	having a pleasant smell; sweet smelling	As Kristen walked through the flower garden, she enjoyed the *fragrant* air.
frail *(adj)* freyl	weak or easily broken	Grandpa's mind is as sharp as ever, but his body is becoming *frail* as he gets older.
gigantic *(adj)* jie-GAN-tik	huge; enormous	Compared to Rhode Island, Texas is a *gigantic* state.
gorgeous *(adj)* GAWR-juhs	magnificent; dazzling; richly or brilliantly colored	The princess wore a *gorgeous* gown to the palace ball.
jagged *(adj)* JAG-id	having sharp points; uneven	We could see *jagged* mountain peaks in the distance.
lanky *(adj)* LANG-kee	awkwardly tall and thin	The once plump child grew into a *lanky* teenager.
scrawny *(adj)* SKRAW-nee	thin and undersized	With proper care and feeding, the *scrawny* puppy soon began to look much healthier.
shabby *(adj)* SHAB-ee	run-down; worn out	The *shabby* old house is in desperate need of repair.
sleek *(adj)* sleek	smooth and shiny	Troy loves to brush his cat's *sleek* fur.
tidy *(adj)* TIE-dee	neat and orderly	Mom wants my room to be *tidy*, but I prefer more relaxed surroundings.

Own It: Develop Your Word Understanding

Box It

Directions: On the five pages that follow, fill in the boxes that surround each vocabulary word. List synonyms and antonyms of the key word, and list nouns that the key word could describe. Finally, sketch or write a memory cue to help you remember the word's meaning.

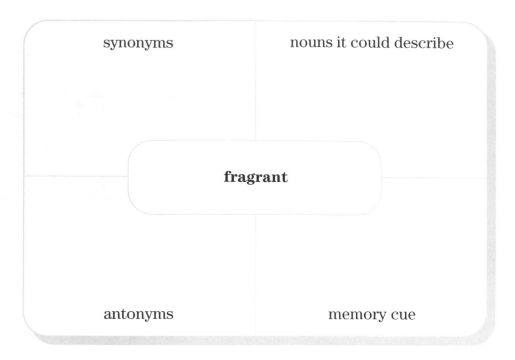

synonyms

nouns it could describe

fragrant

antonyms

memory cue

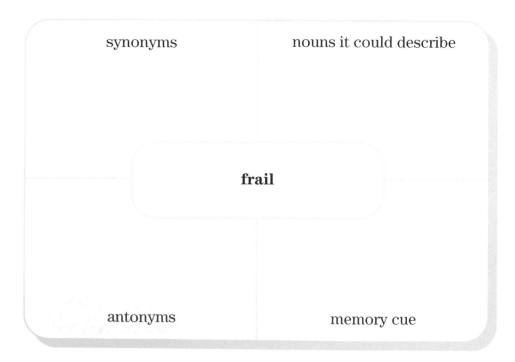

synonyms

nouns it could describe

frail

antonyms

memory cue

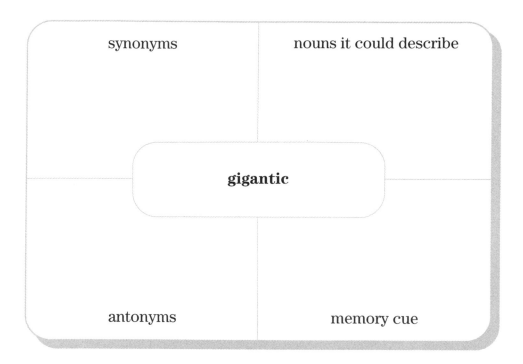

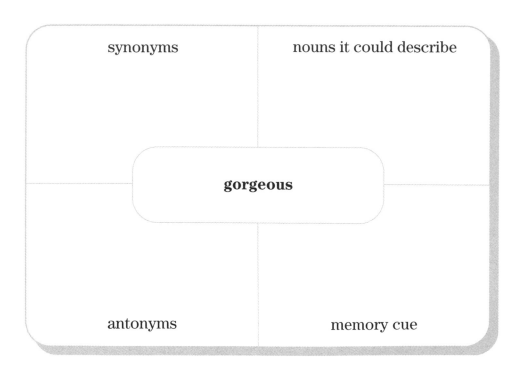

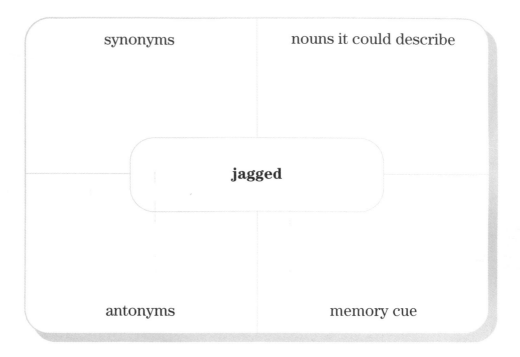

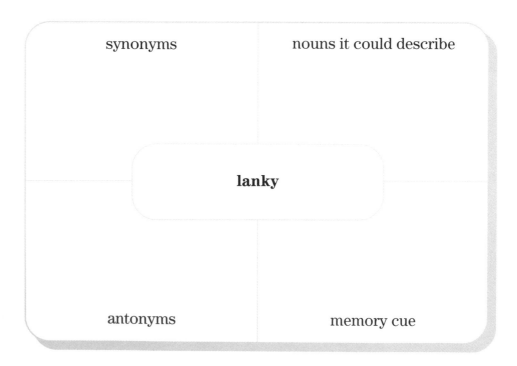

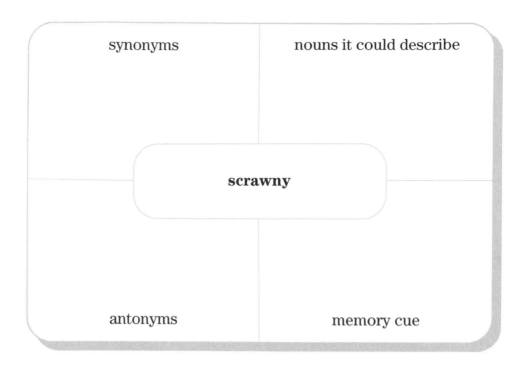

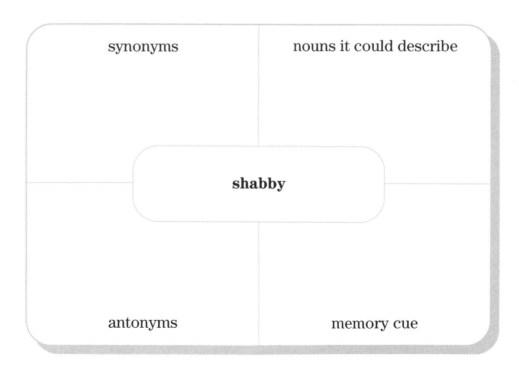

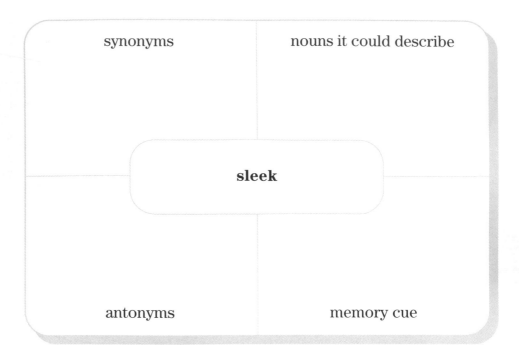

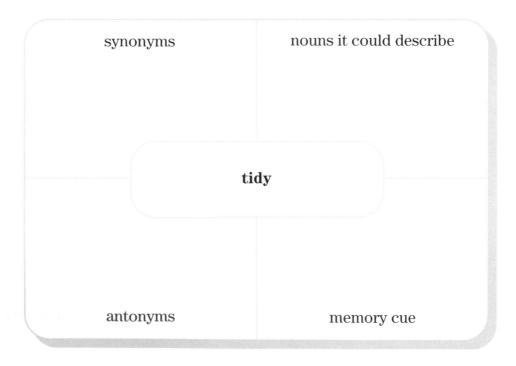

Link It: Make Word-to-World Connections

10 Things I Love About You

Directions: Pick a person and write sentences to describe things you love about him or her. Use all ten vocabulary words from page 187 in your sentences—a task that requires you to get creative. For instance, *shabby* doesn't seem to have positive meaning, so how could you use it to describe something you love about someone? One final note—when you write your list, you can change the person's name to protect your privacy!

Master It: Use Words in Meaningful Ways

Set Me Free—In Verse!

Directions: Free verse is a type of poetry that does not use a set rhyme or rhythm (meter) pattern. Here is an example of free verse. Notice that the lines focus on one main thought, but there is no rhyme or meter.

Heart Problems

You shattered my heart

With a look,

And you injured my spirit

With a word;

You're no friend of mine.

Create your own poem, written in free verse, using some of the vocabulary words. A fun way to start is to take phrases and sentences from your work in the 10 Things I Love About You activity. Edit and rearrange these phrases and sentences to form a poem. Then add the finishing touch: a title. Share your creation with classmates in a poetry festival.

List 30 Words That Describe Behavior and Actions

These ten words (adjectives) describe behavior and actions. Read each word, what it means, and how it's used. As you study each word, think about people (real or from TV, books, and movies) whom you might describe using these words.

Word	What It Means	How It's Used
courteous *(adj)* KUR-tee-uhs	having good manners; polite	Colin is a *courteous* young man who always remembers to say "please" and "thank you."

continued

fatal *(adj)* FAY-tl	resulting in ruin or failure	The chess player's move proved to be a *fatal* error.
feeble *(adj)* FEE-buhl	without force; weak	The silly joke was a *feeble* attempt at humor.
frisky *(adj)* FRIS-kee	playful; lively	After chasing each other around the house, the *frisky* kittens fell asleep.
mischievous *(adj)* MIS-chuh-vuhs	playful but troublesome; naughty	Those *mischievous* children are always playing pranks.
reckless *(adj)* REK-lis	not careful; wild	Police gave the man a ticket for *reckless* driving.
romantic *(adj)* roh-MAN-tik	characterized by feelings of love	The young couple took a *romantic* stroll in the moonlight.
sensible *(adj)* SEN-suh-buhl	showing good sense; wise	Finishing your homework before going to the movies is a *sensible* decision.
triumphant *(adj)* try-UHM-fuhnt	celebrating success or victory; victorious	After winning the match, the tennis player gave a *triumphant* shout.
urgent *(adj)* UR-juhnt	calling for immediate action or attention	The general made an *urgent* appeal for more troops.

Own It: Develop Your Word Understanding

Mix and Match

Directions: In this activity, you will mingle with classmates, trying to match vocabulary words with their definitions. Here's what to do:

1. Your teacher will write each vocabulary word on an index card. On separate cards, he or she will write the definitions. Then the cards will be jumbled together in a box.

2. Pull one card from the box. You'll have a word or a definition.

3. Move around the room to find the person who has the definition of your word, or the word that goes with your definition.

4. With your word-definition partner, write a sentence that uses the vocabulary word. Then identify another form of the word (such as an adverb or a noun form). Share the results in a class discussion.

Link It: Make Word-to-World Connections

I'm Thinking of a Word . . .

Directions: In this activity, you and your classmates will use the vocabulary words to describe things in your own lives. Here's how the activity works:

1. Cut two strips of paper. On each one, write the name of something in your life that could be described by one of the vocabulary words from List 30. For instance, you might write *kitten* on one slip and *phone call* on the other.

2. Your teacher will collect all the slips of paper and jumble them in a box. Then, he or she will pull out one slip and read the word aloud.

3. Students suggest one or more vocabulary words that logically describe the word. (If the word is one of *your* two words, stay silent.)

4. Repeat the process with the next slip of paper pulled from the box.

Master It: Use Words in Meaningful Ways

Passion Club

Directions: What is your passion? Do you love motorcycles or skateboarding or singing? Maybe you are passionate about nature or fashion or softball. In this activity, you'll choose something that you're passionate about and plan a club based on this passion. Here's what to do:

1. Brainstorm a list of all the things you really like—things you're passionate about.

2. Choose one passion that some of your friends would enjoy sharing with you.

3. Plan a "passion club" based on this interest. To plan the club, think about some of these questions: What is the purpose of the club? Who can join? How often will the club meet? What will you do at club meetings? What is the club's name?

4. Create a flyer that announces your club and gives details about it. On the flyer, use at least half of the vocabulary words, or other forms of the words.

5. You can choose to hand out the flyer to your friends, or show it only to your teacher.

Wrapping Up: Review What You've Learned

Here's a brief summary of what you've studied in this chapter.

> Many words have more than one meaning. Familiar words often have less familiar additional meanings.

> Many words have both literal and figurative meanings. *Literal* means using words in their usual, dictionary sense. *Figurative* means using words in an imaginative way that goes beyond their ordinary meanings.

> Writers use figurative meanings to create a certain effect or to paint a mental picture. Figurative language includes similes, metaphors, personification, hyperbole, and irony.

> Such describing words as *good*, *big*, and *nice* give only a general idea of meaning. They are not precise. Use specific descriptive words when you write and speak, in order to get your ideas across more clearly.

Flaunt It: Show Your Word Understanding

In the following exercises, you'll demonstrate your understanding of each vocabulary word. You will use vocabulary words, or forms of the words, to complete sentences and to write sentences of your own.

A Word Bank

Directions: Choose a word from the box to complete each sentence. Write the word on the line provided. Each word may be used only once.

> feeble   conduct   operation   whimper   positive
> epic   fuse   sensible   suspend   fatal

1. If you prefer, you may _____ the interview in the conference room.

2. _____ responses to the test version of the product suggest that the product will be a success.

3. Is it _____ to wear sandals in a blizzard?

4. Yikes! I have a/an _____ amount of homework to do tonight.

5. My mom gets annoyed when I _____ like a puppy to beg for food.

6. The old woman's body was _____, but her mind was still strong and lively.

7. The attack on Fort Sumpter lit the _____ that began the Civil War.

8. To create an interesting effect, you can _____ the paintbrush above the paper, letting drops of paint fall down.

9. Too much salt is _____ to any recipe.

10. The _____ of the sewing machine is easy. I'll explain it to you.

B Sentence Completion

Directions: Circle the letter of the word that best completes each sentence.

11. In the latest _____ of our newsletter, you can find information on joining our club.

    a. element   **b.** epic
    c. reference   **d.** issue

12. The cat had been living alone on the streets for months, and it had grown _____ from lack of food.

    a. scrawny   **b.** sleek

    c. triumphant   **d.** tidy

13. Babysitting for the Jones family was enjoyable, except when the _____ six-year-old locked me out of the house for an hour.

    a. romantic   **b.** mischievous

    c. jagged   **d.** stale

14. A single _____ bee buzzed about in the large flower garden.

    a. courteous   **b.** sly

    c. forlorn   **d.** fragrant

15. The _____ rumors you spread about her were unfair and untrue.

    a. sensible   **b.** toxic

    c. stale   **d.** lanky

C Writing

Directions: Write one or more sentences to answer each of the following questions. Be sure to use the italicized vocabulary word in your sentence. Write your sentences on a separate sheet of paper.

16. What is an event or class for which you would like to *register*?

17. What is something in your house that is *gorgeous*?

18. What is something in your house that is *shabby*?

19. Would you want to adopt a *frail* old dog from an animal shelter?

20. What would you call a monster who had *gigantic* feet?

21. What could happen if you are *reckless* near a swimming pool?

22. What is one thing that *frisky* ponies might do?

23. If you have an *urgent* message for a friend, do you call or do you send a text message?

24. What items do you regularly *deposit* into a recycling bin?

25. When you turn off the lights in your bedroom, what objects *lurk* in the shadows?

Activities à la Carte: Extend Your Word Knowledge

The activities on this page are presented à la carte, like items on a restaurant menu, meaning that you can choose from a variety of options. Your teacher may assign an activity or let you pick the one that tempts your appetite. If time allows, you might do more than one activity. All of the activities feature the same ingredient: **exploring the meanings of words**. Dig in!

Play Me a Tune

Get out the poem you wrote for the Set Me Free—In Verse! activity (page 193) and set it to music. Grab a few musicians, a lead singer, and—voilà!—you've created a band with its first original song.

One Potato, Two Potato

Do multiple-meaning words in this lesson have multiple meanings when translated into another language? Or must you translate the English word into several different words to get the range of meanings? Find out and share your insights with the class.

I've Taken a Shine to You

Idioms are phrases that express a thought figuratively, not literally. That is, you can't understand the phrase by looking up the words in a dictionary. You have to learn what the phrase means within the culture that created it. Create an idiom poster to display in class. List a dozen or so idioms, and explain their meanings. Here are a few to get you started: blind luck, piece of cake, puppy love, fly on the wall, apple of my eye.

But Wait! That's Not All

Some vocabulary words in this chapter have more meanings than those listed here. Often, these additional meanings are associated with different parts of speech. Identify some of these words and tell your class about additional meanings.

Mega-Memory Game

Create a mega-memory card game. You'll need 20 index cards and a list of five words that have more than one meaning. Use four cards per word—on two cards, write the key word; on the other two cards, write two meanings of the word. Shuffle the cards and place them facedown in rows. Invite one or two friends to play. To begin, turn over a card. Then turn over another card. If the two cards contain a word and one of its definitions, you win a point. (Put your winning cards in a stack in front of you.) If the cards don't match, turn them facedown again. Then the next person gets a turn.

On Second Thought

Pull out a piece of writing that you are working on for a class or other project. Pump up the word power in the piece by using descriptive words with clear meanings and by using words figuratively. Then pat yourself on the back for using tools of the trade.

Looks Like a Duck, Sounds Like a Duck

Homonyms are words that are spelled and pronounced the same but have different meanings, such as "Duck your head in the water" and "A duck swims using its webbed feet," and the multiple-meaning words in this chapter. *Homographs* are spelled alike but have different meanings, origins, and sometimes pronunciations. Compare "*Lead* me to my seat" and "The pencil *lead* broke." There are also homophones, words that sound alike but have different spellings and meanings, such as *break* and *brake*. To educate your classmates, create a three-column chart that helps them understand *homonyms*, *homographs*, and *homophones*.

Song in My Heart

Song lyrics are a gold mine when it comes to figurative uses of words. Examine the lyrics of some of your favorite songs, looking for words used figuratively. How does this use of a word fire your imagination, touch your heart, or dazzle your mind's eye?

The One and Only—Or Not

Is English the only language that uses words figuratively? Find out and report back to your classmates. Give them examples from English and the other language to make your explanation clear.

Understanding Shades of Meaning

9

T hink of a person you know who has a way with words. You might say this person has a silver tongue. He or she seems to say the right thing in the right way, smoothly moving through conversations like a ship through calm water. How does this person do it?

In this chapter, you'll learn a few techniques that can give you a way with words. These techniques include using words with positive or negative connotations, choosing (and recognizing) words that send particular messages, and using formal language to your advantage. Who knows—maybe you'll soon become known as "that person with the silver tongue."

Objectives

In this chapter, you will learn

> How a word can seem positive or negative

> How a word can be filled with attitude or bias

> How a word can carry a formal or an informal tone

Sneak Peek: Preview the Lesson

Gut Reactions

In the following questions, some of the italicized words are vocabulary words in this chapter. Answer each question giving your first response, or gut reaction. Don't worry about explaining *why* you answer the way you do. As you complete this lesson, you'll have opportunities to discuss why you might respond to a word in a particular way.

1. Would you rather be described as *ignorant* or *uninformed*?

_____

2. Which is more likely to be a safe group: a *crowd* or a *mob*?

    _____

3. Are the *claims* of advertisements always trustworthy?

    _____

4. If you said to your teacher, "May I *inquire* about what you just said?" would your classmates laugh or not?

    _____

5. If a friend invited you to a party, would you say that you'd *ponder* the invitation or that you'd *think* about it?

    _____

Vocabulary Mini-Lesson: Words Have Feelings

Many words have meanings that are similar but not exactly the same. Compare these sentences:

> Anthony walked into the room.
>
> Anthony strolled into the room.
>
> Anthony wandered into the room.
>
> Anthony marched into the room.

All four sentences describe the same event. Read each sentence again. How does changing one word change the image in your mind?

Here's another example:

> Rena was surprised when she opened the door.
>
> Rena was astonished when she opened the door.
>
> Rena was stunned when she opened the door.
>
> Rena was shocked when she opened the door.

Changing a single word changes your understanding of the sentence. Was Rena happy or unhappy when she opened the door? You can't know for sure, because you don't know exactly what she saw. However, a strong word like *shocked* has a less pleasant feel to it that a mild word like *surprised*. *Shock* is something you probably associate with scary movies and unpleasant news. *Surprise* may make you think of parties and presents. Even though the two words are similar in meaning, one seems to have a *negative* feeling while the other leaves a more *positive* impression.

To talk about the feelings associated with words, you'll find it helpful to understand two terms: denotation and connotation. The **denotation** of a word is its exact, literal meaning (you read about literal meanings on page 177). For example, the denotation of *walk* is "to move along on foot."

In addition to denotations, many (but not all) words have connotations. The **connotation** of a word is the impression the word makes in our mind. It's a feeling that is *suggested* but not stated. For example, look again at the following sentences:

Anthony marched into the room.

Marching into a room has a different connotation from *walking* into a room. *March* suggests that Anthony is feeling a certain way—angry, perhaps?—or else has a definite purpose in mind.

Rena was shocked when she opened the door.

Shocked has a negative connotation. In other words, *shocked* suggests that what Rena is seeing is unpleasant or unfavorable in some way.

Look at these pairs of sentences. What is the denotation of the underlined words? Does each word also have a connotation? If so, do you think the connotation is positive or negative?

Kim is <u>thrifty</u>. Her sister is <u>stingy</u>.

Mom cooked a <u>meal</u>. Dad prepared a <u>feast</u>.

Evan is <u>skinny</u>. His cousin is <u>slim</u>.

James is <u>clever</u>. His friend is <u>sly</u>.

All of the words in List 31 have connotations. Read the example sentences carefully. Use the context to help you understand whether the word has a positive or negative connotation.

ords to Know: Vocabulary Lists and Activities

In this section, you'll study words that have positive or negative connotations.

List 31   Words with Positive and Negative Connotations

Read each word, what it means, and how it's used. Think about each word's positive or negative connotation.

Word	What It Means	How It's Used
absurd *(adj)* ab-SURD	ridiculous; laughable	"The dog ate my homework" is an *absurd* excuse for not handing in an assignment.
cunning *(adj)* KUHN-ing	clever at deceiving; sly	The *cunning* thief avoided capture by tricking the police.
gripping *(adj)* GRIP-ing	holding one's interest or attention	This author writes *gripping* tales of mystery and adventure.

continued

ignorant *(adj)* IG-ner-uhnt	lacking knowledge	Only an *ignorant* voter would support a candidate just because he speaks well.
mature *(adj)* muh-TOOR	having the qualities of full development	Aliya is an excellent babysitter because she is very *mature* for her age.
mob *(n)* mob	a large number of people; crowd	An excited *mob* surrounded the famous singer
scheme *(n)* skeem	a plan of action	Your get-rich-quick *scheme* is sure to get us into trouble.
scribble *(v)* SKRIB-uhl	to write quickly or carelessly	Running out of time, Adam *scribbled* an answer to the last test question.
stimulating *(adj)* STIM-yuh-late-ing	encouraging thought or action; interesting	Shira had a *stimulating* conversation with the two professors.
striking *(adj)* STRY-king	drawing attention; outstanding	The actor's *striking* performance is sure to earn him glowing reviews.

Own It: Develop Your Word Understanding

Connotations

Directions: In a small group, share your ideas about the connotation of each vocabulary word. Start by having one person read a word aloud. Make sure everyone understands the word's meaning. Then tell the group whether the word has mostly positive (pleasant) connotations to you or mostly negative (unpleasant) connotations.

To help one another identify connotations, ask questions such as, "Would you want me to describe your outfit as *absurd*?" and "Would you rather be called *mature* or *immature*?"

In the ten organizers that follow, classify each word's connotation as positive or negative. Then explain *why* you think the word carries mainly pleasant or unpleasant overtones.

> **absurd**
>
> **connotation**

> explanation of connotation

cunning

connotation

explanation of connotation

gripping

connotation

explanation of connotation

ignorant

connotation

explanation of connotation

mature

connotation

explanation of connotation

mob

connotation

explanation of connotation

scheme

connotation

explanation of connotation

scribble

connotation

explanation of connotation

stimulating

connotation

explanation of connotation

striking

connotation

explanation of connotation

Link It: Make Word-to-World Connections

Welcome to My World

Directions: In this activity, you'll work alone and then with a group to link vocabulary words to your world. Here's what to do:

1. Play around with the vocabulary words, using them to make statements about yourself, friends, family members, your neighborhood, or other aspects of your life. Write at least five sentences using vocabulary words.

2. Choose three sentences that best describe your world. Cut your paper in strips, one sentence per strip.

3. In a small group, jumble everyone's sentences in a box. Take turns pulling out a sentence, reading it aloud, and guessing whose life it describes.

Master It: Use Words in Meaningful Ways

Popcorn and Movies

Directions: In this activity, you'll write a movie review to share with classmates. Follow these steps:

1. Choose a movie to review. It could be a movie that's in theaters now, a television movie, a home movie, a video rental—it's up to you. (If you are unable to watch a movie, talk to your teacher about reviewing a book instead.)

2. Watch the movie and take notes as you do so. Keep the vocabulary words from List 31 handy and jot down comments about the movie using these words.

3. Write your movie review. Tell readers what the movie is about (but don't give away the ending!). Point out strong points and weak points of the movie and describe your favorite part.

4. With your teacher, plan a popcorn and movie event in class, where you snack on popcorn while people share their reviews. Afterward, you'll have enough movie recommendations to keep you entertained for a month!

ocabulary Mini-Lesson: Words Contain Messages

Writers choose their words carefully. They know that the connotations of words shape readers' thoughts and opinions. Compare these two sentences:

Mayor Lonnigan is a determined man with bold ideas for our city's future.

Mayor Lonnigan is a stubborn man with reckless ideas for our city's future.

Which sentence do you think was written by a supporter of Mayor Lonnigan? How do you know?

Words like *determined* and *bold* have positive connotations, while *stubborn* and *reckless* have negative connotations. A writer can send a message to readers by choosing the words that express his or her own feelings. Unless you think about the connotations of words, you might not even realize a message is being sent!

Such unspoken messages are everywhere. They appear in newspaper and magazine articles, in TV commercials, and in printed advertisements. Be on the lookout for them. Think carefully about what you read and hear. Watch for words that are meant to win you over or persuade you to act or think in a certain way.

Words to Know: Vocabulary Lists and Activities

The words in List 32 relate to the sending of messages through written and spoken communication. You can use these words when you discuss articles and advertisements. These words will also help you think about the ways people try to persuade one another.

List 32   Words and Messages

Read each word, what it means, and how it's used.

Word	What It Means	How It's Used
campaign (n) kam-PAIN	a group or series of ads or commercials designed to sell a product or products	The company launched an advertising *campaign* to sell sports equipment to teenagers.
claim (n) kleym	a statement presented as fact, which may be questioned	What evidence does the manufacturer offer to support the *claim* that its peanut butter tastes best?
imply (v) im-PLY	to express without stating directly; suggest	The editorial *implies* that the senator has done something wrong.
influence (v) IN-floo-uhns	to have an effect on thought or action; affect	TV commercials *influence* how viewers spend their money.
interpret (v) in-TUR-prit	to explain or understand the meaning of	The politician's vague statement can be *interpreted* in more than one way.
mass media (n) mas MEE-dee-uh	media (see *medium*, below), such as television and newspapers, that can reach large numbers of people	The *mass media* shape people's opinions through words and pictures.
medium (n) MEE-dee-uhm	a method for communicating information over a distance (plural: *media*)	Television is an especially powerful *medium* because so many people own TV sets.

continued

slant *(v)* slahnt	to present in such a way as to express a particular point of view	Through careful choice of words, magazine writers can *slant* their stories.
spin *(n)* spin	a particular way of thinking about something presented for the purpose of shaping opinion	The president tried to put a hopeful *spin* on the report, even though the news was not encouraging.
values *(n)* VAL-yooz	the beliefs, goals, or standards that a person or group of people consider important	Advertisers try to appeal to viewers' *values* when they create television and radio commercials.

Own It: Develop Your Word Understanding

A Few Questions

Directions: In this activity, you'll fill out a questionnaire. To answer the questions, you must understand the meanings of the vocabulary words. Work with a partner if your teacher approves.

Backyards of America

Thank you for volunteering to work for Backyards of America. This campaign will solicit donations of clothing and nonperishable food items. Volunteers must complete the following questionnaire.

1. What person or goal *influenced* your decision to volunteer with us?

_____

2. Have you worked on a charitable *campaign* before? _____

3. How do you *interpret* our motto, "Charity begins in our own backyard"?_____

4. With which *media* would you like to work? (Circle all that apply.)

    television   radio   print   live events

5. With which *medium* would you **most** like to work? _____

6. Are you willing to collect food and clothing for people who do not share your personal or religious *values*? _____

7. Many people are too embarrassed to accept charity. How can we put a more positive *spin* on charity? _____

_____

8. Do you agree with the *claim* that charity makes people greedy? Explain. _____

9. In your opinion, does being poor *imply* laziness? Explain.

_____

10. This campaign is *slanted* toward a young audience. Where can we advertise to reach young people under age 20? _____

_____

Link It: Make Word-to-World Connections

I'm Watching You

Directions: Put mass media under your microscope. For a week, take special notice of what you see, hear, and read in mass media. Share some of your observations and conclusions with the class. To frame your thoughts, you can choose to use some or all of these sentence starters:

Sentence Starters

> An advertising *campaign* that seems convincing/ridiculous is . . .

> A reporter *claims* that . . .

> A commercial *implies* that . . .

> A magazine article *influenced* me to . . .

> As I *interpret* the news story, it means . . .

> The *mass media* seems focused on . . .

> The *medium* that I most enjoyed was . . .

> The TV station's programming is *slanted* toward an interest in . . .

> A celebrity put a positive *spin* on bad behavior by . . .

> Some *values* that this television program teaches are . . .

Master It: Use Words in Meaningful Ways

Ad Campaign

Directions: Imagine that you work for an advertising agency. You must develop an ad campaign for a client's product, and you must present your ideas in a meeting. To prepare for the meeting, follow these steps.

1. Divide a poster board down the center. On one half, you'll create an advertisement for a product of your choosing (shoes, a music CD, food, or the like). On the other half, you'll explain why the advertisement will be *effective* (why it will work).

2. Use art supplies, magazine cutouts, and other materials to create an ad for the product.

3. List five reasons why the ad will be effective. Use some of the List 32 vocabulary words to help express these reasons.

4. Present your poster and ideas in a small group or to the whole class, as directed by your teacher.

Vocabulary Mini-Lesson: Words Carry Tone

When was the last time you wore your fanciest clothes? Maybe you attended a wedding or a special religious ceremony. No doubt, you chose your clothes with care. You didn't just pull on a sweatshirt and an old pair of jeans. You dressed in a way that was appropriate for the occasion.

Language is not so different from clothing. Writers and speakers choose words that are appropriate for the occasion. They choose words that match the **tone**—the expression of mood—of the occasion. For example, let's say you are writing an essay for English about a disagreement that you had with someone. You might describe how the argument "upset" you. You would use a more formal, polished tone since you were writing for the teacher. If you were talking to your best friend, though, you might say you were "bummed out" by what happened. You would use a more casual tone.

Just as you wouldn't wear jeans to a wedding, you wouldn't use slang for a school essay. In the same way, writers don't use chatty, casual language when they create serious documents like reports or business letters. Instead, they choose more formal language. Such language may not always be the simplest way to express ideas. However, it does add "weight" to what is being said. Formal words send an unspoken message: *This is a serious matter.*

Words to Know: Vocabulary Lists and Activities

In the following sections, you'll study a list of words that are appropriate for formal, serious situations.

List 33 Formal Words

Read each word, what it means, and how it's used. In what formal situations might you use these words?

Word	What It Means	How It's Used
caution *(n)* KAW-shuhn	care to avoid risk or danger; watchfulness	Workers must exercise *caution* when operating machinery.
dispute *(n)* di-SPYOOT	disagreement; argument	The two women appeared before a judge to settle their legal *dispute*.
distinguished *(adj)* di-STING-gwisht	famous; outstanding	Professor Bienstock is a *distinguished* scholar who has written many books.

continued

essential *(adj)* uh-SEN-shuhl	so important as to be absolutely necessary	Eating a balanced diet is *essential* to good health.
inquire *(v)* in-KWIRE	to find out information; ask	If you want to *inquire* about this job opening, contact the manager.
ponder *(v)* PON-der	to think over; consider carefully	Scientists *pondered* the results of the experiment.
primary *(adj)* PRY-mer-ee	most important; main	Our *primary* concern is the safety of the children.
request *(n)* ri-KWEST	something asked for	We hope that the bank will grant our *request* for a loan.
resolve *(v)* ri-ZOLV	work out; settle	If both sides are willing to listen, they can *resolve* their disagreement.
sufficient *(adj)* suh-FISH-uhnt	as much as needed; enough	The jury thought the evidence was *sufficient* to prove the man's guilt.

Own It: Develop Your Word Understanding

Eeny Meeny Miney Moe

Directions: Choosing the right word for the occasion is a sign of a well-educated person. In this activity, you'll explore a range of words that can mix and match with the vocabulary words.

Each vocabulary word is listed in the Formal column. In the Informal column, write one or more informal synonyms. Two samples are provided. You may work with a partner.

Formal Word	Informal Synonyms
caution	*carefulness*
dispute	*argument, fight, spat*
distinguished	
essential	
inquire	

continued

Formal Word	Informal Synonyms
ponder	
primary	
request	
resolve	
sufficient	

Link It: Make Word-to-World Connections

In Other Words

Directions: In this activity, you'll express one thought in two ways: formally and informally. With a partner, follow these steps:

1. Talk about when you have used the vocabulary words or the related informal synonyms. Help each other understand any words whose meanings are still unclear.

2. In the list of vocabulary words (pages 212–213), look at the third column, How It's Used. Your task is to rewrite each example sentence using an informal synonym instead of the formal vocabulary word.

3. Read some of your new sentences aloud to the class.

Master It: Use Words in Meaningful Ways

In All Seriousness

Directions: Rules govern our lives at school, work, and play, no matter our age. Some rules are fair and necessary; others may be unfair or unnecessary. Think of a rule that seems unfair or unnecessary to you. Write a formal letter to the person who enforces this rule, explaining why you think the rule is not needed. In your letter, use at least four vocabulary words (or forms of them). Deliver the letter if you wish.

Wrapping Up: Review What You've Learned

Here's a summary of what you've studied in this chapter.

> Many words have meanings that are similar but not exactly the same. Often when two words have similar meanings, one of the words seems to have a negative feeling while the other leaves a more positive impression.

> The **denotation** of a word is its exact, literal meaning. Many words also have connotations. The **connotation** is the impression or feeling the word creates in our mind.

> By choosing a word with a certain connotation, the writer can change the reader's understanding of the sentence.

> Writers choose their words carefully because they know that the connotations of words shape readers' thoughts and opinions. A writer can send an unspoken message—positive or negative—by choosing words that express his or her own feelings.

> Writers and speakers choose words that are appropriate for the occasion. When serious language is called for, they don't use chatty, casual language. Instead, they use more formal language that adds weight to what is being said.

Chapter Review Exercises

Flaunt It: Show Your Word Understanding

In the following exercises, you'll demonstrate your understanding of each vocabulary word. You will use vocabulary words, or forms of the words, to complete sentences and to write sentences of your own.

A Sentence Completion

Directions: Circle the letter of the word that best completes each sentence.

1. When I said that I had spoken to a Martian, Mrs. Gregory said, "That's _____."

   a. mature **b.** primary
   c. absurd **d.** essential

2. My _____ plan for a surprise party worked fabulously. My sister never suspected a thing.

   a. cunning **b.** scheme
   c. ignorant **d.** sufficient

3. If you would apologize to me, then we could _____ this unpleasant matter.

   a. inquire **b.** ponder
   c. interpret **d.** resolve

4. I'd like you to write an article on moving to a new city, and please _____ it toward a pleasant view of moving.

   a. slant **b.** imply
   c. scribble **d.** influence

5. During student council election week, I made fifteen _____ posters.

   a. medium **b.** spin
   c. mass media **d.** campaign

B Word Choice

Directions: Underline the word that best completes each sentence.

6. Standing atop a cliff was the (*slant, striking*) figure of a wolf, dark against the moon.

7. The chief (*claim, caution*) in Tim's report is that *The Wednesday Wars* by Gary D. Schmidt is the best book you'll ever read.

8. After a heated (*dispute, request*), the two friends became enemies.

9. I am so proud of my brother, a (*gripping, distinguished*) Boy Scout.

10. Police were sent to deal with the (*mob, mass media*) that had formed in front of the mayor's office.

C Writing

Directions: Follow the directions to write sentences using vocabulary words, or forms of the words. Write your sentences on a separate sheet of paper.

11. Use *stimulating* in a description of something that you read.

12. Use *values* to tell something about yourself.

13. Use *mature* to express an opinion.

14. Use *imply* to ask a question.

15. Use *caution* in an imperative sentence (a sentence that makes a command).

Activities à la Carte: Extend Your Word Knowledge

The activities on this page are presented à la carte, like items on a restaurant menu, meaning that you can choose from a variety of options. Your teacher may assign an activity or let you pick the one that tempts your appetite. If time allows, you might do more than one activity. All of the activities feature the same ingredient: **shades of meaning in words**. Dig in!

Wordplay

Some people invent secret codes, and others learn the slang of new friends. Some people buy boxes of magnetic words and arrange them into poems on the refrigerator. Why? People like to play with the shades of meaning in words. Choose an art form and play with some words of your choosing. You might make a collage of words ripped from newspaper headlines, for example, or print words from this chapter and adorn them with images that they inspire. Display your wordplay in your classroom.

Environmental Print

For a week, keep an observation notebook about environmental print. This is the writing that you see on signs, notices, billboards, banners, menus, and other printed matter in public places. Which examples use formal language? Which use informal language? Do any signs carry "unspoken messages"? Do any signs use words with strong negative or positive connotations, or are the words neutral? Share your findings with your class.

Kindly Join Me

Host a formal dinner party for your friends. Set a dress code, plan a seating arrangement, and create a set of "conversation cards" to break the ice. On each card, write a question that can be read aloud to the group to get a conversation started. Be sure to use vocabulary words from this chapter on your conversation cards!

 ### What Did You Just Say?

A professional translator must master not only a second language but also connotations of words in that language. Find out about the career path of translation and report back to your class. What kinds of jobs can a translator get? Why is connotation so important to the job of translation?

Subtext

Mass media are masters at using *subtext*, or messages hidden "under" the stated message. To study this phenomenon, look for an advertisement that says one thing but implies another thing. (For instance, does a shampoo ad imply that your hair is unattractive if you don't use the shampoo?) Using vocabulary words in this chapter, explain both the obvious message and the subtext, or hidden message, in the ad you studied.

Spinmaster

In the 1990s, a sitcom called *Spin City* got laughs for its stories of a deputy mayor who had to put a positive spin on the mayor's embarrassing behavior. Use vocabulary words in this chapter to inspire your own sitcom—perhaps a boy who always puts a positive spin on his twin's misbehavior, or a group of students who put a positive spin on the eccentric behavior of a beloved teacher. Develop a cast of characters for your sitcom and write a plot outline that describes the main idea of the show.

Encore! Encore!

In this book, you've studied scores of vocabulary words. Which words confounded you? Delighted you? Inspired you? Choose 52 words and use them to create a Word of the Week calendar. You can recycle an old calendar by pasting new paper in it, use scrap paper and a hole punch, or design and print out pages. For each word, give a pronunciation guide, a definition, and an example sentence.

Appendix A

Using a Dictionary

A dictionary entry usually gives you the following information about a word:

> The pronunciation and how it's divided into syllables. The pronunciation is either given as a respelling, which shows you how to sound out the word (as done in this book), or it is given using what are called diacritical marks, or symbols. (Dictionaries with diacritical marks have keys that show you what those marks mean.) Hyphens or spaces show how a word is divided into syllables.

> The part of speech.

> The different definitions, sometimes with sample phrases or sentences

> Other forms of the word parts of speech

> Synonyms.

pan•ic (PAH-nik)

Etymology: from the Greek *panikos*, of Pan

Date: 17th century

panic *(n)* **1** a sudden fright or terror **2** *slang:* person who is very funny

Synonym: see *fear*

—**panicky** *(adj)*

panic *(v)* to behave as if scared

Dictionary Sources

Following is a list of some of the many dictionary sources available to you.

Free Online Dictionaries

> **Merriam-Webster Online**. www.m-w.com. This site contains a dictionary, a thesaurus, a Spanish/English dictionary, and audio pronunciations.

> **Dictionary.com**. www.dictionary.com. Here you can find a dictionary, a thesaurus, audio pronunciations, a reference tool, and a translation tool with more than 30 languages.

> **Yourdictionary.com**. www.yourdictionary.com. This site's features include audio pronunciations, synonyms, and usage examples.

Dictionary Subscriptions

> **Oxford English Dictionary**. www.oed.com. Available by paid subscription online or on CD-ROM.

> **Merriam-Webster Unabridged Dictionary**. www.m-w.com. This online dictionary, available by paid subscription, contains more definitions than Merriam-Webster's free online dictionary.

Print Dictionaries

Check your local bookstore or an online store like Amazon to see all the different kinds of dictionaries available to you. Here are two of the most basic and widely used dictionaries.

> *The Merriam-Webster English Dictionary*
> *Concise Oxford English Dictionary*

Glossary

A

aboard (uh-BAWRD) *(adv)*: on a ship, airplane, or other vehicle

absurd (ab-SURD) *(adj)*: ridiculous; laughable

academy (uh-KAD-uh-mee) *(n)*: a school, especially a private high school

acquire (uh-KWY-r) *(v)*: to come to have; get

activate (AK-tuh-vayt) *(v)*: *to* make active

adept (uh-DEPT) *(adj)*: being highly trained or skilled, or having expertise

admiral (AD-mer-uhl) *(n)*: the commanding officer of a navy

adobe (uh-DOH-bee) *(n)*: sun-dried brick

affectionately (uh-FEK-shuhn-it-lee) *(adv)*: with warm, loving feelings (affection)

afloat (uh-FLOHT) *(adv)*: floating

allege (uh-LEJ) *(v)*: to state or claim something before proving or without proving

allergy (AL-er-jee) *(n)*: unusual reaction to a particular substance, such as a food, pollen, or dust

amazement (uh-MAYZ-ment) *(n)*: condition of being amazed

analyze (AN-l-ize) *(v)*: to examine or study

antifreeze (AN-ti-freez) *(n)*: a substance added to a liquid to keep it from freezing

antiwar (AN-ti-wawr) *(adj)*: against war or against a particular war

archaeology (ahr-kee-OL-uh-jee) *(n)*: the scientific study of past life and culture

architecture (AHR-ki-tek-cher) *(n)*: the art or science of designing and constructing buildings

ashore (uh-SHOR) *(adv)*: to or on the shore

asthma (AZ-muh) *(n)*: disease characterized by breathing difficulty, wheezing, and coughing

attitude (AT-i-tood) *(n)*: way of acting, thinking, or feeling

attorney (uh-TUR-nee) *(n)*: a lawyer

attorney general (uh-TUR-nee JEN-er-uhl) *(n)*: the chief law officer of a nation or state

autobiography (aw-tuh-by-AH-gruh-fee) *(n)*: a person's biography (life story) written by the person himself or herself

autograph (AW-tuh-graf) *(n)*: a person's handwritten signature

automatic (aw-tuh-MAT-ik) *(adj)*: acting or moving by itself

automatically (aw-tuh-MAT-ik-lee) *(adv)*: by itself

B

ballet (ba-LAY) *(n)*: an artistic form of dance

banister (BAN-uh-ster) *(n)*: a handrail of a staircase

barista (bahr-EE-stuh) *(n)*: a person who makes and serves coffee drinks for customers

barometer (buh-ROM-i-ter) *(n)*: instrument for measuring the pressure of the atmosphere

biography (bye-OG-ruh-fee) *(n)*: a written account of a person's life

boredom (BOAR-duhm) *(n)*: state or condition of being bored

bouquet (boo-KAY) *(n)*: a bunch of flowers

brochure (broh-SHOOR) *(n)*: a pamphlet

bronze (bronz) *(n)*: a metallic mixture of copper and tin

C

calico (KAL-i-ko) *(n)*: a cotton fabric

campaign (kam-PAIN) *(n)*: a group or series of advertisements or commercials designed to sell a product or group of products

caution (KAW-shuhn) *(n)*: care to avoid risk or danger; watchfulness

charity (CHAR-i-tee) *(n)*: the giving of money or service to those in need

civilized (SIV-uh-lahyzd) *(adj)*: characterized by good taste, manners, and refinement

claim (kleym) *(n)*: a statement presented as fact, which may be questioned

clash (klash) *(v)*: to come into conflict

classical (KLAS-i-kuhl) *(adj)*: relating to the art, literature, and culture of ancient Greece and Rome

clockwise (KLOK-wize) *(adv)*: in the direction in which the hands of a clock move

colorless (KUHL-er-lis) *(adj)*: without color

compose (come-POZE) *(v)*: to form by putting together

concept (KON-sept) *(n)*: idea or thought

condemn (kuhn-DEM) *(v)*: to announce to be wrong or evil (especially to pronounce guilty in law)

conduct (kuhn-DUHKT) *(v)*: to show the way; lead; to direct the performance of; to direct or manage; carry out

conservation (kon-ser-VAY-shuhn) *(n)*: careful management and protection of natural resources and the environment

contentment (kuhn-TENT-muhnt) *(n)*: condition of being content; satisfaction

contract (KON-trakt) *(n)*: an agreement between two or more people

contribute (kon-TRIH-byoot) *(v)*: to give together

conveniently (KUHN-veen-yuhnt-lee) *(adv)*: in a way that is easy to use or get to

courageous (kuh-RAY-juhs) *(adj)*: having courage

courteous (KUR-tee-uhs) *(adj)*: having good manners; polite

cunning (KUHN-ing) *(adj)*: clever at deceiving; sly

cybercrime (SIGH-ber-krime) *(n)*: criminal activities carried out through the use of computers or the Internet

D

deposit (di-POZ-it) *(v)*: to place for safekeeping; to put down; leave behind

derrick (DER-ik) *(n)*: a large crane used to lift and move heavy objects

diagonal (die-AG-uh-nl) *(n)*: extending on a slant between opposite points

dialogue (DAHY-uh-lawg) *(n)*: a conversation between two or more people

diameter (die-AM-i-ter) *(n)*: a straight line passing through the center of a circle from one side to the other

diesel (DEE-zuhl) *(n)*: a type of engine that burns fuel oil

dispute (di-SPYOOT) *(n)*: disagreement; argument

distinguished (di-STING-gwisht) *(adj)*: famous; outstanding

doubtful (DOUT-fuhl) *(adj)*: having doubt

downward (DOUN-werd) *(adv)*: toward a lower place or position

duffel (DUH-full) *(n)*: a rough, heavy woolen material

duplicate (DOO-pli-kayt) *(v)*: to make a copy of

duration (doo-RAY-shuhn) *(n)*: the time during which something lasts

E

edutainment (ej-oo-TAYN-muhnt) *(n)*: entertainment (TV shows, movies, games) that are meant to be educational

element (EL-uh-muhnt) *(n)*: one of the basic substances from which all matter is made up; a part or quality

encouragement (en-KUR-ij-ment) *(n)*: action of encouraging

engaged (en-GAYJD) *(adj)*: involved or interested in

epic (EP-ik) *(adj)*: a long narrative that tells about someone's heroic deeds, or something in history that would be worthy of such a narrative

erupt (e-RUHPT) *(v)*: to burst forth

essential (uh-SEN-shuhl) *(adj)*: so important as to be absolutely necessary

evaporate (i-VAP-uh-rayt) *(v)*: to make into vapor; to change from a liquid or solid into vapor

exhale (eks-HAYL) *(v)*: to breathe out

export (ik-SPAWRT) *(v)*: to carry or send to another country

exporter (EK-spawrt-er) *(n)*: a country that sells goods to another country

expose (ik-SPOZE) *(v)*: to make known; reveal

F

fanatic (fuh-NAT-ik) *(n)*: someone who is overly or unreasonably excited

fantabulous (fan-TAB-yuh-luhs) *(adj)*: (blend of *fantastic* and *fabulous*) outstandingly good; excellent

farsighted (FAHR-sigh-tid) *(adj)*: better able to see distant objects than objects nearby

fatal (FAY-tl) *(adj)*: resulting in ruin or failure

feeble (FEE-buhl) *(adj)*: without force; weak

felony (FEL-uh-nee) *(n)*: a serious crime for which the punishment may be a prison sentence of more than one year, or even death

fever (FEE-ver) *(n)*: a body temperature that is higher than normal

finance (fi-NANS) *(v)*: to provide money for

forefront (FAWR-fruhnt) *(n)*: position of greatest importance or activity; leading position

forlorn (fawr-LAWRN) *(adj)*: sad and lonely

fossil fuels (FOS-uhl FEW-uhlz) *(n)*: fuels such as coal, gas, and oil, used as an energy source

fragrant (FRAY-gruhnt) *(adj)*: having a pleasant smell; sweet-smelling

frail (freyl) *(adj)*: weak or easily broken

freedom (FREE-duhm) *(n)*: state or condition of being free

frisky (FRIS-kee) *(adj)*: playful; lively

fuse (fyooz) *(n)*: a cord, wick, or other device used to set off an explosive charge; a safety device placed in an electric circuit to protect against dangerous overload

G

gauze (gawz) *(n)*: a thin, lightweight cloth

geocentric (jee-oh-SEN-trik) *(adj)*: having Earth as its center

geology (jee-OL-uh-jee) *(n)*: the scientific study of the earth

gigantic (jie-GAN-tik) *(adj)*: huge; enormous

ginormous (jih-NOR-muhs) *(adj)*: (blend of *gigantic* and *enormous*) extremely large

global warming (GLOWH-bul WORE-ming) *(n)*: a gradual increase in Earth's temperature, generally believed to be caused by pollution

golden (GOHL-duhn) *(adj)*: made of or like gold

google (GOO-gul) *(v)*: to use the Google search engine to find information about someone or something on the World Wide Web

gorgeous (GAWR-juhs) *(adj)*: magnificent; dazzling; richly or brilliantly colored

gracious (GRAY-shuhs) *(adj)*: having grace

grave (greyv) *(adj)*: very serious

gripping (GRIP-ing) *(adj)*: holding one's interest or attention

H

hazmat (HAS-matt) *(adj)*: (short for *hazardous material*) dangerous substances

heliocentric (hee-lee-oh-SEN-trik) *(adj)*: having the sun as its center

herculean (hur-kyuh-LEE-uhn) *(adj)*: very difficult or challenging

high-def (high-DEF) *(adj)*: (short for *high-definition*) a system that offers high-quality images with greater detail than standard images

hideous (HID-ee-uhs) *(adj)*: ugly; horrible

humanism (HYOO-muh-niz-uhm) *(n)*: the idea that each person is special and has great worth in the world

hurriedly (HUR-eed-lee) *(adv)*: in a hurry or rush; quickly

hygiene (HIGH-jeen) *(n)*: practices that help to ensure good health, such as cleanliness

hypnosis (hip-NOH-sis) *(n)*: a trancelike state in which (some people believe) a person is more easily influenced by others

I

icon (EYE-kon) *(n)*: a symbol or picture

ignorant (IG-ner-uhnt) *(adj)*: lacking knowledge

immigrant (IM-ih-grant) *(n)*: a person who immigrates (comes to a new country)

imply (im-PLY) *(v)*: to express without stating directly; suggest

impose (im-POZE) *(v)*: to push or force into being; to push into the notice or company of someone

inaccurate (in-AK-yer-it) *(adj)*: not accurate; incorrect

inactive (in-AK-tiv) *(adj)*: not active or moving

inconsiderately (in-kuhn-SID-er-it-lee) *(adv)*: without consideration for others; thoughtlessly

incredibly (in-KRED-uh-blee) *(adv)*: in a way that is hard to believe

indefinitely (in-DEF-uh-nit-lee) *(adv)*: without limit; endlessly

influence (IN-floo-uhns) *(v)*: to have an effect on thought or action; affect

informal (in–FAWR-muhl) *(adj)*: not formal; casual; relaxed

inhabitant (in-HAB-i-tuhnt) *(n)*: a person or animal that inhabits (lives in) a place

inquire (in-KWIRE) *(v)*: to find out information; ask

inscribe (in-SKRAHYB) *(v)*: to write or engrave (cut or carve)

interfere (in-ter-FEER) *(v)*: to come between; get involved in the affairs of others

internal (in-TUR-nl) *(adj)*: of or arising within a person or being (In medicine, *internal* can specifically mean given or applied by being swallowed.)

international (in-ter-NASH-uh-nl) *(adj)*: between or among nations

internationally (in-ter-NASH-uh-nl-ee) *(adv)*: among nations; worldwide

Internet (IN-ter-net) *(n)*: the worldwide network of computers

interpret (in-TUR-prit) *(v)*: to explain or understand the meaning of

irritate (IR-i-tayt) *(v)*: to cause to feel angry or annoyed

issue (ISH-oo) *(n)*: a topic to be considered or discussed; something sent out or published

J

jagged (JAG-id) *(adj)*: having sharp points; uneven

judgment (JUHJ-ment) *(n)*: result of judging

jury (JOOR-ee) *(n)*: a group of citizens chosen to serve in a court of law and give a decision based on the evidence presented

K

kilometer (kil-OM-i-ter) *(n)*: a unit of length equal to 1,000 meters

L

lanky (LANG-kee) *(adj)*: awkwardly tall and thin

legalize (LEE-guh-lahyz) *(v)*: to make legal, or permitted by law

lengthwise (LENGKTH-wize) *(adv)*: in the direction of the length

lurk (lurk) *(v)*: to lie hidden but waiting, especially for evil purposes

M

magnify (MAG-nuh-fie) *(v)*: to make great or large

mammoth (MAM-uhth) *(n)*: an extinct mammal of the elephant family

manager (MAN-i-jer) *(n)*: person who manages

manuscript (MAN-yuh-skript) *(n)*: handwritten or typewritten document

marine (muh-REEN) *(adj)*: relating to the sea

martial (MAHR-shuhl) *(adj)*: of, relating to, or suggestive of war or a warrior; warlike

mass media (mas MEE-dee-uh) *(n)*: media (see *medium*), such as television and newspapers, that can reach large numbers of people

mature (muh-TOOR) *(adj)*: having the qualities of full development

medieval (mee-dee-EE-vuhl) *(adj)*: of the Middle Ages

medium (MEE-dee-uhm) *(n)*: a method for communicating information over a distance (plural: *media*)

microscope (MY-kruh-skohp) *(n)*: an instrument for making tiny objects appear larger

Midas touch (MY-duhs tuhch) *(n)*: someone who has an ability to make money very easily in any area he/she enters into

mirage (mi-RAHZH) *(n)*: an optical illusion in which a person imagines seeing something that isn't there

misbehave (mis-bi-HAYV) *(v)*: to behave badly

mischievous (MIS-chuh-vuhs) *(adj)*: playful but troublesome; naughty

miscommunication (mis-kuh-MYOO-ni-kayh-shun) *(n)*: unclear or incorrect communication

mispronounce (mis-pruh-NOWNCE) *(v)*: to pronounce incorrectly

misstatement (mis-STEYT-muhnt) *(n)*: incorrect statement

misunderstand (mis-uhn-der-STAND) *(v)*: to understand incorrectly; get the wrong idea

mnemonic (ni-MON-ik) *(adj)*: assisting or helping memory

mob (mob) *(n)*: a large number of people; crowd

moisten (MOY-suhn) *(v)*: to make moist

mysteriously (mi-STEER-ee-uhs-lee) *(adv)*: in a way that is difficult to understand or explain

N

narrator (NAR-ay-ter) *(n)*: person who narrates

natural resources (NACH-er-uhl REE-sawrs-ez) *(n)*: materials provided by nature that people use or eat

nearsighted (NEER-sigh-tid) *(adj)*: better able to see objects that are nearby than objects at a distance

nonrenewable resources (NON-ri-NOO-a-buhl REE-sawrs-ez) *(n)*: natural resources that cannot be replaced once used

O

obsession (uhb-SESH-uhn) *(n)*: an idea or activity that occupies too much of a person's attention

ogre (OH-ger) *(n)*: in fairy tales and folklore, a giant or monster

online (ON-LAHYN) *(adv, adj)*: through a computer network

operation (op-uh-RAY-shuhn) *(n)*: a medical procedure done to the body, usually with instruments, for the purpose of restoring health; way of working; action performed by military or government forces

opponent (uh-POH-nuhnt) *(n)*: a person who opposes (goes against) another, as in a game or contest

P

painful (PAYN-fuhl) *(adj)*: full of pain

panic (PAN-ik) *(n)*: sudden, intense fear

pedestal (PED-uh-stl) *(n)*: a base supporting a column; also, a stand for displaying a statue or sculpture

pedestrian (puh-DES-tree-uhn) *(n)*: a person traveling on foot

pedometer (puh-DOM-i-ter) *(n)*: an instrument that records the distance that a person walks

periscope (PER-uh-skohp) *(n)*: an instrument for seeing objects that are outside the viewer's direct line of sight

perspective (per-SPEK-tiv) *(n)*: a point of view

petty (PET-ee) *(adj)*: having no importance or minor importance

photograph (FOH-tuh-graf) *(n)*: a picture taken with a camera

plea (plee) *(n)*: something that is alleged or begged in defense, or as an excuse; a genuine request for help or sympathy

ponder (PON-der) *(v)*: to think over; consider carefully

popularize (POP-yuh-luh-rahyz) *(v)*: to make popular

portable (PAWR-tuh-buhl) *(adj)*: that can be carried or easily moved

positive (POZ-i-tiv) *(adj)*: not open to question; certain; indicating that someone approves, agrees, or accepts

prescription (pri-SKRIP-shuhn) *(n)*: a doctor's written directions for the preparation and use of a medicine

primary (PRY-mer-ee) *(adj)*: most important; main

proclaim (proh-KLAME) *(v)*: to declare publicly

promote (pruh-MOHT) *(v)*: to raise in position or rank

proponent (pruh-POH-nuhnt) *(n)*: someone who argues in favor of something; supporter

provoke (pruh-VOHK) *(v)*: to stir up; bring forth; cause

psyche (SIGH-kee) *(n)*: mind or soul

publicly (PUHB-lik-lee) *(adv)*: in a public way; openly

purify (PYOOR-uh-fie) *(v)*: to make pure

python (PIE-thon) *(n)*: a large snake found in Africa, Asia, and Australia

R

radically (RAD-ik-lee) *(adv)*: basically; completely

reactivate (ree-AK-tuh-vayt) *(v)*: to make active again

reassure (ree-uh-SHUR) *(v)*: to assure again; give confidence to

reckless (REK-lis) *(adj)*: not careful; wild

reclassify (ree-KLAS-uh-fie) *(v)*: to assign to a different category

recluse (REK-loos) *(n)*: someone who leads a solitary life

reference (REF-er-enss) *(n)*: the directing of attention to; source of information; a person who can provide information about or a recommendation for another

reformer (ri-FAWR-mer) *(n)*: a person who tries to bring about political or social reform, or improvement

register (REJ-uh-ster) *(v)*: to enter one's name in a record; to indicate; show

Renaissance (ren-uh-SAHNS) *(n)*: historical period during which there was new interest in ancient Greek and Roman culture

renewable resources (ri-NOO-a-BUHL REE-sawrs-ez) *(n)*: natural resources that nature can replace as they are used

replacement (ri-PLAYS-muhnt) *(n)*: a person or thing that takes the place of another

replenish (ri-PLEN-ish) *(v)*: to fill up again or stock up

request (ri-KWEST) *(n)*: something asked for

resident (REZ-i-duhnt) *(n)*: a person who resides (lives in) a place

resolve (ri-ZOLV) *(v)*: work out; settle

reverse (ri-VURS) *(adj)*: opposite in position or direction

revise (ri-VIZE) *(v)*: to read over and improve or correct as needed

revive (ri-VIVE) *(v)*: to bring back to life or consciousness

revolve (ri-VOLV) *(v)*: to move in a path around; circle

romantic (roh-MAN-tik) *(adj)*: characterized by romance or feelings of love

S

safari (suh-FAHR-ee) *(n)*: a journey or hunting expedition

saxophone (SAK-suh-fohn) *(n)*: a woodwind instrument

scheme (skeem) *(n)*: a plan of action

scrawny (SKRAW-nee) *(adj)*: thin and undersized

scribble (SKRIB-uhl) *(v)*: to write quickly or carelessly

search engine (surch EN-juhn) *(n)*: computer software used to search for information on the Web

secular (SEK-yuh-ler) *(adj)*: relating to worldly things; not religious

seismograph (SIZE-muh-graf) *(n)*: an instrument for recording how strong an earthquake is and how long it goes on

sensible (SEN-suh-buhl) *(adj)*: showing good sense; wise

shabby (SHAB-ee) *(adj)*: run-down; worn out

shawl (shawl) *(n)*: a cloth worn as a covering for the head or shoulders

sideburns (SIDE-burnz) *(n)*: hair on the sides of the face

silken (SIL-kuhn) *(adj)*: like silk

sitcom (SIT-kom) *(n)*: (short for *situation comedy*) a comedy series that involves the same cast of characters in a succession of episodes

skyward (SKY-werd) *(adv)*: toward the sky

slant (slahnt) *(v)*: to present in such a way as to express a particular point of view

sleek (sleek) *(adj)*: smooth and shiny

sleepless (SLEEP-lis) *(adj)*: without sleep

sly (slahy) *(adj)*: clever and sneaky

sofa (SOH-fuh) *(n)*: a couch

souvenir (soo-vuh-NEER) *(n)*: something kept as a reminder

space shuttle (speys SHUHT-l) *(n)*: a spacecraft designed for shuttling people and equipment between Earth and a space station

spacious (SPAY-shuhs) *(adj)*: full of space

spam (spam) *(n)*: worthless e-mail, usually advertisements, sent to large numbers of people

spin (spin) *(n)*: a particular way of thinking about something presented for the purpose of shaping opinion

sprain (spreyn) *(n)*: an injury to a ligament (tissue that connects bones) by twisting or wrenching

stale (steyl) *(adj)*: dry and tasteless as a result of having been kept too long

stimulating (STIM-yuh-late-ing) *(adj)*: encouraging thought or action; interesting

strengthen (STRENGK-thuhn) *(v)*: to make strong

striking (STRY-king) *(adj)*: drawing attention; outstanding

strive (strahyv) *(adj)*: to put forth a great deal of energy or effort

submarine (suhb-muh-REEN) *(n)*: a vessel designed to operate under water

submerge (suhb-MURJ) *(v)*: to put or go under water

sufficient (suh-FISH-uhnt) *(adj)*: as much as needed; enough

supercross (SOO-per-kross) *(n)*: a motorcycle race that includes high jumps and is usually held on a dirt track indoors

surf (surf) *(v)*: to browse or scan, looking for something of interest

suspend (suh-SPEND) *(v)*: to cause to stop temporarily; to hold in place from above; hang

symptom (SIMP-tuhm) *(n)*: a condition that indicates or results from a disease or other disorder

T

tangerine (tan-juh-REEN) *(n)*: a sweet, juicy citrus fruit

tearfully (TEER-fuh-lee) *(adv)*: with tears

telecommunication (tel-i-kuh-myoo-ni-KAY-shuhn) *(n)*: electronic communication over long distances

telescope (TEL-uh-skohp) *(n)*: instrument for viewing distant objects

testify (TES-tuh-fie) *(v)*: to make sworn statements in a court of law

thoughtless (THAWT-lis) *(adj)*: without thought

thoughtlessly (THAWT-lis-lee) *(adv)*: without thought or consideration for others

tidy (TIE-dee) *(adj)*: neat and orderly

tornado (tawr-NAY-doh) *(n)*: a violently whirling windstorm, usually appearing as a dark, funnel-shaped cloud

toxic (TOK-sik) *(adj)*: containing poison

transformation (trans-fer-MAY-shuhn) *(n)*: change

transmit (trans-MIT) *(v)*: to send or pass along from one place or person to another

transparent (trans-PAR-uhnt) *(adj)*: letting light through so that objects on the other side can be seen

trespass (TRES-pass) *(v)*: to enter another person's land or property without the person's permission

trial (TRY-uhl) *(n)*: a formal examination of a case in a court of law to determine whether the charge or claim made is true

triumphant (try-UHM-fuhnt) *(adj)*: celebrating success or victory; victorious

truce (troos) *(n)*: an agreement that calls the end to fighting

typhoon (tie-FOON) *(n)*: a violent tropical windstorm

U

unconscious (uhn-KON-shuss) *(adj)*: not conscious

underestimate (uhn-der-ES-tuh-mayt) *(v)*: to estimate too low; place too low a value on

underpay (uhn-der-PAY) *(v)*: to pay too little

underpayment (uhn-der-PAY-muhnt) *(n)*: too little payment

uneventful (uhn-i-VENT-fuhl) *(adj)*: without any noteworthy events

ungracious (uhn-GRAY-shuhs) *(adj)*: not gracious; rude

unsolved (uhn-SAHL-ved) *(adj)*: not solved; without explanation

unsuccessfully (uhn-suhk-SES-fuhl-ee) *(adv)*: without success

unwelcome (uhn-WELL-kuhm) *(adj)*: not wanted or welcome

uphold (uhp-HOHLD) *(v)*: to support or keep up

upward (UHP-werd) *(adv)*: toward a higher place or position

urgent (UR-juhnt) *(adj)*: calling for immediate action or attention

utterly (UHT-er-lee) *(adv)*: absolutely; totally

V

vague (vayg) *(adj)*: not clear or exact

values (VAL-yooz) *(n)*: the beliefs, goals, or standards that a person or group of people consider important

verdict (VUR-dikt) *(n)*: the decision of a judge or jury

verify (VER-uh-fie) *(v)*: to check for accuracy

W

ward (wawrd) *(n)*: a division in a hospital, usually where patients with a similar condition are treated

watt (wot) *(n)*: a unit of electric or mechanical power

Web (web) *(n)*: (short for *World Wide Web*) a system of interconnected Internet sites, offering text, graphics, and sound

whimper (HWIM-per) *(v)*: to make a low cry or sound that expresses displeasure

wireless (WIRE-lis) *(adj)*: operating without needing to be connected with wires

witness (WIT-nis) *(n)*: a person who makes sworn statements in court as to what he or she has seen or heard

Y

yacht (yot) *(n)*: a boat for pleasure cruising or racing

Z

zoology (zoh-OL-uh-jee) *(n)*: the scientific study of animals

Index